W9-CME-949

THE ALLEGHENY

Books by Frederick Way, Jr.

THE LOG OF THE BETSY ANN
PILOTIN' COMES NATURAL

Rivers of America books already published are:

KENNEBEC by Robert P. Tristram Coffin
UPPER MISSISSIPPI (New Revised Edition, 1944) by Walter Havighurst
SUWANNEE RIVER by Cecile Hulse Matschat
POWDER RIVER by Struthers Burt
THE JAMES (New Revised Edition, 1945) by Blair Niles
THE HUDSON by Carl Carmer
THE SACRAMENTO by Julian Dana
THE WABASH by William E. Wilson
THE ARKANSAS by Clyde Brion Davis
THE DELAWARE by Harry Emerson Wildes
THE ILLINOIS by James Gray
THE KAW by Floyd Benjamin Streeter
THE BRANDYWINE by Henry Seidel Canby
THE CHARLES by Arthur Bernon Tourtellot
THE KENTUCKY by T. D. Clark
THE SANGAMON by Edgar Lee Masters
THE ALLEGHENY by Frederick Way, Jr.
THE WISCONSIN by August Derleth
LOWER MISSISSIPPI by Hodding Carter
THE ST. LAWRENCE by Henry Beston
THE CHICAGO by Harry Hansen
TWIN RIVERS: *The Raritan and the Passaic,* by Harry Emerson Wildes
THE HUMBOLDT by Dale L. Morgan
THE ST. JOHNS by Branch Cabell and A. J. Hanna
RIVERS OF THE EASTERN SHORE by Hulbert Footner
THE MISSOURI by Stanley Vestal
THE SALINAS by Anne B. Fisher
THE SHENANDOAH by Julia Davis
THE HOUSATONIC by Chard Powers Smith
THE COLORADO by Frank Waters
THE TENNESSEE: THE OLD RIVER, *Frontier to Secession* by Donald Davidson
THE CONNECTICUT by Walter Hard
THE EVERGLADES by Marjory Stoneman Douglas

SONGS OF THE RIVERS OF AMERICA, edited by Carl Carmer

THE
RIVERS OF AMERICA

Edited by
STEPHEN VINCENT BENÉT
and CARL CARMER

As Planned and Started by
CONSTANCE LINDSAY SKINNER

Art Editor
FAITH BALL

THE ALLEGHENY

by

FREDERICK WAY, JR.

Illustrated by

HENRY PITZ

RINEHART & COMPANY, INC.

New York *Toronto*

PRINTED IN THE UNITED STATES OF AMERICA
BY THE HADDON CRAFTSMEN, INC., SCRANTON, PA.

In so far as I am able to ascertain, these persons are the only living beings, aside from myself, who have come down the Allegheny River from Olean, New York, to Pittsburgh, Pennsylvania, in a motorboat.

Bud Morrison
Jim Way
Woody Rutter
Jimmy Ague
Fred Way III
Bill Gray
Sand Bar Johnny Zenn

To these modern pioneers this volume is affectionately dedicated.

THE ALLEGHENY

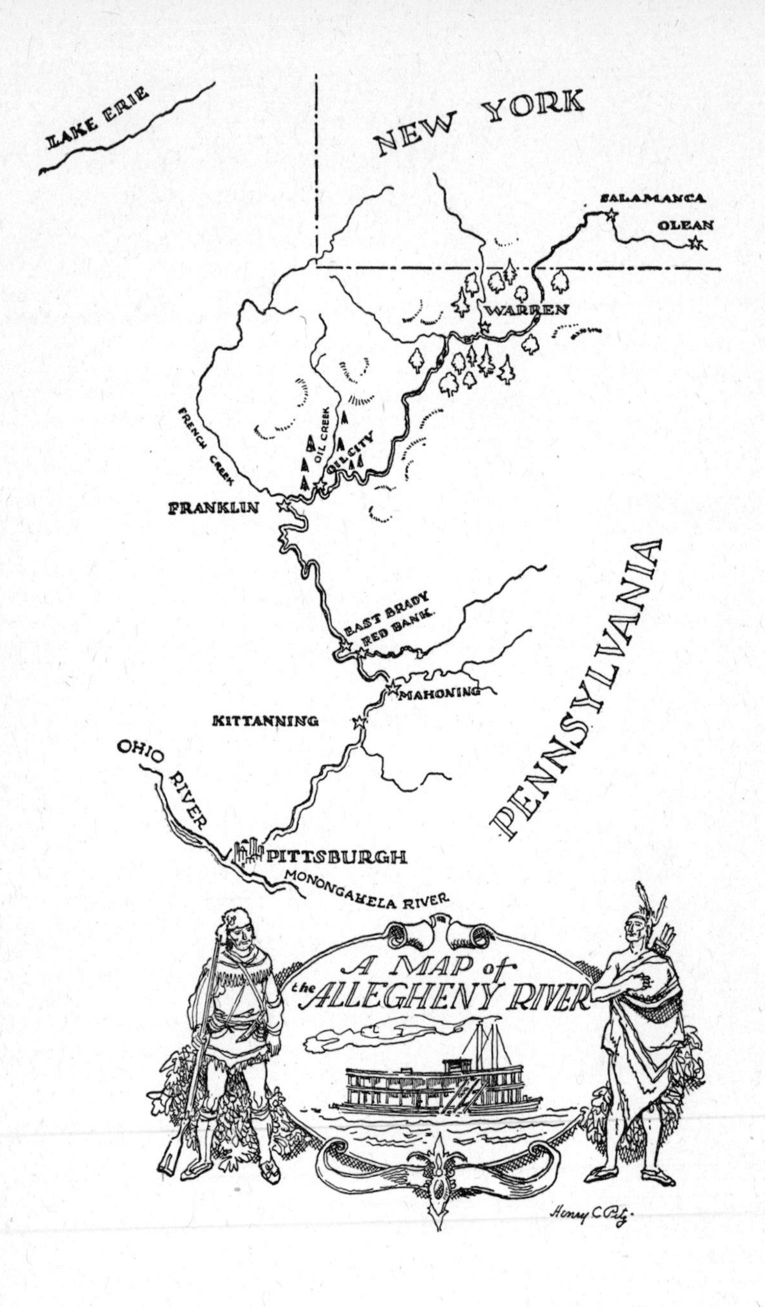
LAKE ERIE
NEW YORK
SALAMANCA
OLEAN
WARREN
FRENCH CREEK
OIL CREEK
OIL CITY
FRANKLIN
PENNSYLVANIA
EAST BRADY
RED BANK
MAHONING
KITTANNING
OHIO RIVER
PITTSBURGH
MONONGAHELA RIVER
A MAP of the ALLEGHENY RIVER
Henry C. Pitz

CHAPTER ONE

IF YOU had a postcard map of the eastern rivers of the United States you would discover a town named Olean, New York, up in the northeast corner, about in the location where you'd normally stick a postage stamp. This town of over 21,000 people is the head of navigation for the Allegheny, Ohio, and Mississippi rivers. Not an idle boast, either, for steamboats have been up there in times past—some 250 miles up the winding, twisting Allegheny. It is a faraway place, and few rivermen have ever been there. Olean has never heard a steamboat whistle for the peculiar reason that the whistle was invented after the last steamboat left there over a hundred years ago. Yet a deal of clear river water flows under the highway bridge away up there in New York, which soon mingles with other streams and becomes broader, and deeper, and after jumping over several hundred riffles, and passing around some 130 islands and 35 towheads and bars, it gets down to a place where there are locks and dams, government lights, buoys, and steamboats and barges. But what a time it has getting there!

We have come to accept, geographically, that the Ohio River is formed by the junction of the Monongahela and Allegheny rivers down there at the "Point" in Pittsburgh. Actually, though, the Allegheny River merely picks up a tributary—as the Monongahela River contributes to a major stream which already has been developed, and grown well out of infancy, and is about to the long-pants stage by the time it gets to the Manchester Bridge, Pittsburgh. The Allegheny River has reached maturity when it picks up the Monongahela—and does it in a matter-of-fact way—same as it already has picked up the Clarion River, French Creek, the Conewango, Oil Creek, and others. In dead low water times the Allegheny puts 650 cubic feet per second into the Ohio; the Monon trickles a mere 160. There has been agitation in times past to rename the Allegheny—to erase that title and call it the Ohio River clear up to the source. Such a change would add 325 miles to the Ohio. But having lately come down this

Allegheny River in a rowboat from Olean, and having observed it, there are two navigators who will vote an emphatic *no* to the idea of a change of name. Let it always be the Allegheny! Will you hear some of our reasons?

There are hundreds of rivermen who have gazed up the Allegheny River and have remarked, "Someday I'd like to go up there and come down in a skiff." It is a mysterious sort of place, and vague tales come wafting down from explorers who have been up there, of boundless fish, primitive forests, majestic mountains, and queer names like Kinzua, Tionesta, Tidioute, and Corydon. We hear of summer camps, and oil country. A glance at a map discloses an Indian reservation bordering the shores. Wild country—adventurous country! Boulders big as a pilothouse and thundering rapids! People getting upset out of small boats in treacherous currents and—as happened in one case—airplanes scouring the river for the bodies in inaccessible places where there are no railroads, highways, or means of getting in. Desolation and eagles' nests. Pine trees atop rugged cliffs. Bears and wolves and ducks so tame they will not move or fly until you can nearly hit their tails with an oar! Inquisitive deer standing along the shores looking at a white man for the first time! A strange place, indeed, this big Allegheny River. Strange and untamed and little explored. Curious that such a place should exist so close to civilization and still be untouched. Miles and miles of pioneer river with absolutely no sign of human handiwork. This, in a part, is the Allegheny. The Ohio River is not like this; neither is the Monongahela. Neither is the Beaver, nor the Muskingum. The Allegheny River is a breed of its own, and it should remain so!

The two adventurers who "cast off" from Olean, New York, on a cloudy, cold morning in mid-May, 1938, with Pittsburgh as their goal, were "babes in the wood" in many respects. Two innocents letting themselves in for whatever came as respected a winding, twisting, writhing mountain stream so remote and wild that no data have been assembled in the United States Engineers Office concerning it for the bulk of its length. The Allegheny at Olean does, actually, look like a river. It has already found a considerable volume of water down there in north central Pennsylvania and on its northwesterly course up into New York State. But rowboat navigation above Olean is next to impossible because of a marshy, boggy country where the water spreads out through myriad shoals and a labyrinth of shallow bars. At Olean it focuses again and firmly resolves to become a river. There is a highway bridge there with a river gauge on its central pier. We got our first qualm when we observed this gauge to discover it was two feet out of water; and our discomfort and anxiety were increased by reason of the fact that we could not read the figures on the gauge because they have been untended and have become illegible. A big creek with many evidences of shoal water. People standing on the banks wagging their heads and predicting dire things. "Too low." "You can't make it."

"Piling across the river a mile below here that you can't get through—like a fine-tooth comb—will wreck your boat when the current dashes you down on them."

"It's been done in a canoe, which can be lifted out of the water at this low stage—but nobody ever brought an eighteen-foot yawl away up here to try the trip—how much does that skiff weigh?"

"About four hundred pounds," replied my partner, Fred Morrison—an adventure-loving youth who was skipping college classes to "be in" on this voyage; his fondness for out-of-door life, snakes, toads, and sundry other crawling and creeping things of the earth made lively visions dance before his mind's eye. He couldn't have stayed in school with this going on; not he. Then he added, "Without the baggage or us, of course."

A man stopped mowing grass at the waterworks and came down to the riverbank where we were launching our boat. He took off his hat and scratched his head. "Pardon me for butting in," he said, "but I've called a newspaper reporter; this looks like news to me. How much does that boat draw?"

We confessed to ten inches—and it sounded and looked as impracticable as though the *Queen Mary* were lying at Fort Benton, Montana, and had steam up, and expected to go down the Missouri with about two feet on the marks.

"Where'd you come from?" somebody asked.

"Down near Pittsburgh."

"How'd you ever get that big boat up here?"

"Shipped it up on the Pennsylvania Railroad."

"That's an uncommon big boat—ain't it—for up here?"

Fred Morrison (whom we will call Bud hereafter, for that is his name to me) and I glanced around and were startled to observe there was no rowboat, johnboat, canoe, or any other description of floating craft in sight. Nobody used them up this way—river too treacherous! We weren't to see any sort of boat for many, many miles.

We stowed the camping equipment away, put our outboard motor on the bottom of the skiff as we saw all too clearly it would be useless, and finally got around to the point of "tapping out for departure."

The newspaper reporter came whizzing over the bridge at the last moment, and a congregation of Girl Scouts paused on the bridge for this uncommon sight of two persons embarking on such a crazy scheme.

"Where do you expect your trouble to start?" inquired the reporter with rankling candor.

"What trouble?"

"Why, you're bound to have trouble—how about right there?" and he pointed his pencil toward a riffle where rocks were strewn through the channel in abandon and bottom was clearly visible for a considerable stretch.

Our boat's name was *Lady Grace*, and my wife, for whom it was named, stood on the shore. She saw an opportune moment and asked privately, "Well, do you still intend to go?"

Bud and I smiled in the affirmative. Good-byes

were said, and we plied the oars with determination right out to the middle of the stream to get properly headed down into the first rapids. *Lady Grace* swung around and pointed downstream. Water roared and tumbled. The current caught the eighteen-foot yawl and carried it forward with increasing speed as the river narrowed into a mere trough. Six miles an hour—soon eight miles an hour—the Girl Scouts ran down the riverbank after us, and couldn't keep up—we were spinning along at breakneck speed and the bottom of the river was slipping along under us with alarming rapidity. Bud and I braced ourselves as we saw big rocks poke their bald heads within an inch or so of the surface to all sides. Roar and tumble!

"Look out!" cried Bud. "Big rock dead ahead!"

A few strokes of an oar—a push with another oar—and we grazed a big brown boulder and left green paint on it from the bottom of the boat. It went by us with the speed of a comet.

"We've made it!" Deep water again—deep as we could reach with an oar. A pool about a half mile long. So we rigged up the outboard motor and soon had it putting and spluttering and had a regular motorboat in operation before we got out of the city limits. People heard this little gasoline motor and came running to the riverbank. "Motorboat!" The exclamation went up and natives gaped at this contraption of ours—which had bold lettering on the stern thwart: LADY GRACE OF SEWICKLEY, PENNA. Bound for Pittsburgh! Our first riffle safely behind.

A cold mountain rain set in—a "mist," as they call it up that way—and a frigid wind came with it. Undaunted we putted on. Then—with no warning whatever—bang!

We'd hit a submerged rock with the propeller, and sheared a pin. Time out for repairs. Hip boots came into play now—wading around on a rock bottom fixing things. Actually the bottom of the Allegheny, for the entire length of 250 miles from Olean to Pittsburgh is rock and gravel. No mud bottoms up in that swift stream.

Caution was the watchword after that minor accident, and we used the oars much of the time all day whenever we met a "boiling" stretch of water, which was most of the time. Slipping along with the clunk-clunk of oarlocks echoing in the hills and crags.

After a lapse of one hundred years a mechanically powered boat was coming down the Allegheny!

CHAPTER TWO

"OH, LOOK!" I exclaimed. Down ahead, on a gravel point, two deer stood eying us. We put up the oars and floated toward them. They sipped water and watched us. Down we came, right on them, and when about a steamboat length away they whisked up the bank and were gone!

"Why didn't you get a picture of that?" asked Bud.

It dawned on me in an instant what "buck fever" meant, because I'd just had a bad case of it. The chance of a lifetime for a wonderful camera shot had gone by—neither of us had even thought of it! The charm of the picture captivated and paralyzed.

A blackening sky, more rain, and wind. Thermometer down to that chilling point of 40, which is worse than freezing for open-weather work. Thunder rumbled in the mountaintops.

"Island ahead!"

We paused and looked. An ominous tumble and roar of rapids caught our ears again, and we could see foaming spume dash over rocks on both sides of a pretty, quiet, wooded island plumb in the middle of the river.

"Which side?" called Bud.

He asked this with the normal idea that I was a steamboat pilot and would know about such things. Well, before leaving, my old pilot-partner, Bill Pollock, told me to stop and float above any island that was in doubt and the current would carry us to the deepest water. But a stiff wind was blowing, so this advice was useless.

"This side looks best," we both said at once, and pointed to both sides—Bud indicating to the starboard, and my finger aiming to port.

"Might toss a quarter," I suggested half aloud. But the river made up our minds for us. All those upper Allegheny islands have a long-pointed gravel bar extending upstream from them, same as on any other well-managed river, and the water sheds off it to either side like rain running off a barn roof. We got over a little to the starboard and soon found ourselves headed down that side whether or no. The channel took an abrupt turn right in the head of the island and threw the whole force of the current plumb down on a pile of rocks. Immediately below the rocks were tree snags with water tearing through the jagged limbs and churning the whole of the scene into something like an egg beater working full steam in a mess of egg-white. "Good-bye, forever," I thought. Somehow, someway, which will never be clearly distinct, we got through with only two bashes and the boat turned completely around three times and one rock hit broadside as fair as you could imagine—and as we went over with a crash I remember seeing a wealth of green paint left on top of that rock—more decoration gone from the bottom of our boat. Any persons contemplating repeating this trip can watch for rocks with green paint on top and avoid them—they draw less than ten inches.

The great absorption of all the human faculties in negotiating this sort of primitive stream makes time pass with incredible rapidity. We were startled to discover it was four o'clock in the afternoon and we hadn't given a thought to stopping for lunch. At five o'clock we sighted the highway bridge at Salamanca, New York, and tied up there. Still raining, and dismal, and getting colder by the minute.

A good hotel room looked good to us that night. No camping in such a place as this. We stowed our baggage in a garage and left the *Lady Grace* riding the swells just above the bridge with a congregation of curious spectators, holding umbrellas over their heads, looking at a skiff which had actually been on the Ohio River—200 miles away—and was bound to see it again a week later. We sent a telegram: "Arrived Salamanca at five all is well." I had a notion to write "Cuff" for the last word, but my wife wouldn't have understood it. "Cuff" on the end of a telegram was the code word for "Everything going nicely" for the boats in the Pittsburgh-Cincinnati trade ever since the time of the *Queen City, Virginia,* and *Keystone State.* "Cuff": we were in a hotel for the night. And a cold rain beat down.

We had resolved to keep count of the islands as we went along, and make record of the side we took, and the condition of the channel—as information for any other scatterbrained idiots who might, for some confusing reason, wish to try this voyage. It was impracticable to do so. There were too many islands. We would have wasted hours every day trying to record our findings—although our intentions were of the best. Our notations started out like this:

"Island just above Salamanca: Went down the left side alongside a row of piling on the left shore—old piling which was evidently put there to form some sort of a dike—and which extended for a quarter of a mile or more. Deep water in close to this piling all the way down; top of the piling at a constant level—about two feet out of the water. NOTE: Left hand side is the wrong side to come down now—although it was once the channel side. Next time come down the right side, although it does not appear so from above. Very shallow rapids and rock below the island make crossing over to Salamanca wharf almost impossible the way we came down—rubbed and hit bottom all the way across."

We might have kept this record up and made quite a volume of information about what we learned—but things were happening too quickly, and there was no time for notebook jotting. Two pairs of eyes were none too many to watch that river and navigate an 18-foot boat over it. Our tabulations were soon reduced to marking an X with a lead pencil on the side of the boat every time we passed an island. When we got out to Lock Number 9 we counted these marks and discovered we had come by 105 islands! This did not count the score or more above Salamanca where we were shooting rapids and keeping a firm toehold to keep from being pitched overboard.

The natural pools—some of them quite deep—lengthen out below Salamanca and by the time we crossed the state line into Pennsylvania the river had grown noticeably. This growth was evident both in width and in volume of water. It brought fresh hazards in that the rapids had more force to them and the rocks seemed to get bigger. Our baby river was growing up. Every island was a real one—usually wooded with forest trees and cluttered with a wealth of wild foliage. The season of the year was about three weeks behind Pittsburgh and vicinity—we discovered it was early spring all over again and the trilliums and dogwood were out, and lilac bushes were bursting with bloom; although at Pittsburgh we had left roses in bud and the season generally well advanced.

Our camping trip started in earnest below Salamanca, as we were in a wild country. Cornplanter Indians watched us with fixed and intent interest as we glided along past their shacks and wooden houses.

"Dinnertime!" I announced to Bud. "Get out the grub."

He looked under the forward hatch, and turned around to announce: "It's gone! Somebody stole all our food while we were in Salamanca!"

Fifty miles from nowhere and not a bite to eat.

We sighted a fisherman. "Where's a store?" we yodeled.

"This is Sunday," he commented. "Ain't no store open on a Sunday."

"Gee whiz," I said.

"Feller named Holt—old raftboat pilot—runs a store down below Quaker Bridge a couple of miles down—might get something there. He's mighty particular about opening up on a Sunday though," said the fisherman.

But Mr. Holt was at home, and he did open up, and that array of cans looked good to us. We stocked up again, and did so amid a running conversation of raftboating; Mr. Holt had floated big white-pine rafts clear out to Parkersburg, West Virginia, down the Ohio. He had a gleam in his old eyes. "For a nickel I'd go along with you boys," he said.

It seemed incredible that we were swashing down

a river which bore a considerable commerce in years past. Right down over these same dashing waves at one time came log rafts—valuable logs of white pine—some of these rafts fully 75 feet wide and from 175 to 200 feet long; the bulk of them went out to Warren, Pennsylvania, and occasionally to Parkers Landing. A steamboat or two had paddled up over these same shoals a century ago. Daylight navigation only, for too much treachery lurked for the dim visibility of night. One old-time raft pilot is said to have run at night, and we asked Mr. Holt about this.

"It's claimed—yes. They say Seth Warren used to heap up a pile of rocks on his raft; when it'd come right dark he'd throw 'em in and listen to the plunk; and know by the sound where he was at. —But I doubt it." And he smiled skeptically.

That night we camped on an island and went to sleep to the tune of frog croakings and the steady roar of rapids below. In the inky blackness of a narrow river guarded by precipitous mountains at either side I lay there and mused for a time about Seth Warren going down plunking rocks and listening to the sound. He was a cousin of Paul Bunyan's, I think.

Below Warren next afternoon we made a mistake and fetched down the wrong side of an island. The water got thinner and finally gave out. We looked around and noticed a big catfish—a dull mossy-looking old veteran—leaning on a rock with his head on his elbows watching us.

"Where's the channel around here?" I asked him.

He merely regarded us without any indication of whether he found us amusing or repulsive.

"You'd think that his years of experience would teach him where the channel is, anyhow," I allowed—loud enough for him to overhear.

We tried to move *Lady Grace*, but she was stuck solid on the bottom, and would not budge in any direction. The catfish watched this, and scratched a whisker.

"Looks like he didn't know much," observed Bud.

Just then we were startled to hear it say, in a catty voice, "I may be dumb but I ain't stuck like you are!" and with that he gave a flip of his tail and swam away at a lively clip.

We had to get out and push *Lady Grace* back up through the shallow riffle we had lately come down; back up over the head of the island bar, and after a half hour of straining we had about six inches of water under the hull and were back in the proper channel. We didn't see a stuck catfish the whole length of the river; they "learned" under good guidance—from those ancient raftboat pilots.

CHAPTER THREE

NEW YORK's big Chautauqua Lake drains into the Allegheny River through Conewango Creek, which comes in at Warren. One dull winter day in 1868 a huge wooden store boat drifted into Madison, Indiana—away down the Ohio River between Cincinnati and Louisville—and the local river-news reporter came down and made inquiry as to details. "We come from Jamestown, New York," said H. Brown, the proprietor. Actually this unwieldy craft had been brought down out of this Conewango Creek—had jumped several dams—and went down the Allegheny and the Ohio. More remarkable was her big cargo: 100,000 panes of window sash, 2,500 frame doors, 1,500 window blinds, and other goods "too numerous to mention." She had been eight months from her starting point when she tied up at the Madison wharf. A fellow named Netherland over at Spring Creek, Kentucky, bought the boat and Mr. Brown returned to New York. This is an example of one of the numberless impossibilities which have actually happened.

The most notorious feat which originated on the Allegheny River was when Paul Boynton got into a rubber suit at Oil City in early March, 1879, and floated out to New Orleans. Narrowest shave: when he went over the falls at Louisville.

Perhaps the craziest stunt on record is when a fellow greased himself up, donned a bathing suit, and swam from Warren to Pittsburgh—191 miles. This was several years ago. He claimed to have swum down through all the riffles, and eyewitnesses say his sore, swollen legs looked the part.

After French Creek and Oil Creek have contributed their waters to the Allegheny at Franklin and Oil City, respectively, the stream commences to look like the upper stretches of the Monongahela—or very like the Ohio below Moundsville. Still a primitive river, however, with no channel lights on the bridges. Away up at Warren there is a floating sand and gravel dipper dredge and some barges. Oil City is honored by a similar, but more elaborate outfit. A fine, clear stretch of deep water above Oil City for several miles: first big, deep piece of river we encountered. A well-kept boathouse there too, and an elaborate clubhouse.

We peeked up Oil Creek and barely had time to realize that oil was once barged out from Titusville—how they did it is a major mystery; and up French Creek, which has heard the 'scape of a steamboat clear up to Meadville; items of historical interest which are all but forgotten, and are vague and meaningless unless a person has actually gazed up the mouths of these small streams which do not look navigable even through a magnifying glass.

Below Franklin the pools become more frequent, and deep, and long. The sun played hide and seek with us as we went around tremendous bends. Wild, still, and scented with cool and fragrant forest shrubs. An occasional ptt-ptt-ptt from a hard-working oil well. The bulk of the islands were bars now, with no trees on them: long, clean gravel bars. Twenty or thirty of these in some 50 miles.

A big rock on a point—initials and names carved in it—one said in bold letters six inches high, SETH RANDOLPH, and was dated in the 1860's. This particular name set me to guessing. "Dayt" Randolph, famous Ohio River pilot who recently died at Reedsville, Ohio, told me about his father being a rafter from the Allegheny River. Possible—yes, barely possible that this Seth Randolph was Dayton's father. The father bringing out rafts of white pine; the son handling the *Queen City* and the *Keystone State*, big Ohio River packets. Many beginnings up in this Allegheny valley: from here sprang the Rees family, the Rodgers tribe, famed in Pittsburgh history.

Below East Brady we watched with some enthusiasm for Dam Number 9 and slack water. We slipped down along the huge timber dike at Red Bank, sounding about eight inches of water the full of its length, and Bud pointed— There it was. A mass of concrete construction clear across the river. Progress had climbed up, or else we had floated down to progress. "Below there it will be easy sailing," we concluded. But too soon.

A figure of a man was silhouetted high on a concrete pier. His arms were waving. His voice came floating up the river to us. "Go back—don't come down any further!" In sheer perplexity we let the current carry us along.

"River's blocked—you can't get through!"

For a fact, the York Construction Company had built piers across the Allegheny in such a way that navigation for even a canoe was impossible; that dam was a barrier of no mean proportions. We had come down from dreamland to present-day reality. Behind, far, far behind, were the deer and bears and Cornplanter Indians. Bleak hillsides now: no more pine and oak. And a modern dam planted square across the river. Sixty-two miles to Pittsburgh.

We eased to shore alongside some piling at the dam. "Have to go back where you came from," said the workman. "Can't go through here—all the river is ripping down through a spillway that'd wreck your boat."

Then a busy little fellow in hip boots appeared. "What's going on here?" he asked. Our story was soon related.

"Well, now, that's something—and we'll discover some way to get you across," said this fellow, who turned out to be E. W. Wolfe, superintendent of construction. "Unload your boat and we'll take you around on a truck."

Twenty minutes later we were in the river again on the lower side of the lock. "First boat through Number Nine," commented Mr. Wolfe, "even if we did have to hitchhike you through."

Our spirits were bolstered considerably over this feat, and they went up another ten points when we aimed the *Lady Grace's* prow downstream—and discovered it pointing on a nice, white, fresh-looking government light. It was like Columbus discovering America.

From then on we had easy going, as we were in the hands of the lockmasters. Joe Zerr welcomed us at his well-ordered Lock Number 8 and filled up our jugs with fresh water. At Locks 7, 6, 5, 4, 3, and 2 we were passed right along with cheery words and a friendly spirit.

One week and several hours after leaving Olean, Bud called out, "I see the Gulf Building." In an afternoon haze it loomed up ahead like a tower of Babylon.

We landed at R. C. Price's boathouse above the Sixth Street bridge, Pittsburgh, and made a telephone call.

"This is us, Grace. . . . We're in Pittsburgh. . . . We've decided to bring the *Lady Grace* on out to Sewickley—be home in an hour."

"There'll be a good supper ready," said a welcome voice—a very welcome voice.

And we kept the appointment.

CHAPTER FOUR

AN APOLOGY is in order.

Lady Grace has popped and spluttered through three chapters; she seems to have done so with sublime disregard of the *history* of the Allegheny River. She has been reprimanded, and bows her prow in shame, and swears she meant well—says she was trying to get the reader acquainted with the *nature* of the Allegheny. That is a dingy excuse maybe, but it comes from a crippled motorboat. *Lady Grace* needs a new bottom. Her good solid cedar hull took a trimming from those grandpa mossback rocks she rammed on the way out. The underside of her hull was a beautiful delicate green at first: now it resembles a flattened-out coconut, shreds and all. Mr. Price, who knows more about boat-fixing than anybody in Pittsburgh, said nothing short of a major operation will make *Lady Grace* serviceable again.

While coming down the Allegheny, Bud Morrison and I wondered and talked about how the first explorers must have acted, and talked, and did, especially as they did not know where they were headed. We speculated as to *who* first saw that beautiful valley. I wonder?

Doubtless this primitive fellow, whoever he was, came upon the shores of the Allegheny River by accident. Like as not he knelt down, took a drink out of it,

said "yum" maybe, and smacked his lips. He may have been tracking a deer, or an elk, or a herd of buffalo. Oddly enough, there are no guarantees connected with this man's race or tribe. He may have been an Indian. Also, he may not have been. Certainly he was no relation to the tribes of Indians which inhabited the Allegheny valley when the first white men started exploring around; these latter-day Indians knew, and said, that there was a tribe of persons long before their time. Curious large piles of dirt abounded through the region, obviously man-made, to which the Delaware Indians shrugged and pointed.

The Delawares knew about a prior Indian tribe of the Allegheny valley called the Allegawes—also they knew these Allegawes were no hands to heap dirt up into enormous piles higher than the trees. Somebody before their time had done the jobs. "Mound builders" they have been called, for lack of a better name.

The name Allegheny, by the way, was derived from this tribe of Allegawes.

The records are not much more convincing when we try to determine who was the first white man to view the Allegheny River. We can speculate, though; no harm in that. His name was Kinney, I think (contraction of Conoconneque), obviously French, and a great trapper. Doubtless he saw the stream in the vicinity of Olean, New York, having come down from one of the New York lakes. He and an Indian guide were good friends, and they followed a well-tracked trail which had been used for generations—perhaps a buffalo trail. Kinney wasn't looking for a river to discover; he was looking for beaver pelts.

"Where's this river go to?" Kinney asked his Indian friend.

"Allegawe, Allegawe, Allegawe," responded the redface, brushing the subject into discard with a wave of his arm.

This is very unsatisfactory history, but how can it be

helped? Kinney didn't act like an explorer or a discoverer; neither, apparently, did his contemporary Indians, or the Indians before them, or the Mound Builders—or *their* great-grandfathers (for surely they must have had them). Not a single soul, up to this time, had shed tears of overwhelming emotion, or planted a flag, or taken possession of the stream, and the streams into which it flows, and all their little streams ad infinitum. This is because two ingredients were lacking in those early, primitive times—soldiers and whisky. You can't sack down a cargo of facts until you get those two items established.

But, cheer up, the fog is lifting—already I can feel the warmth of the summer sun. This is morning in the Allegheny River's career, and a heavy fog bids for a fair and sparkling day.

Before we get to the year 1669, which properly may be called "The Year of the Big Argument," let us gather up all the crumbs of the Allegheny River's ancient history and sweep them under the carpet once and for all. But look closely among these crumbs, for herein is to be found an event which eclipses anything else chronicled concerning the Allegheny regions. Sometime after man's arrival on the North American continent (some 20,000 years ago, more or less) a series of glaciers enveloped practically all of Canada and the upper portions of the United States. Nobody knows why this happened. Someday some fellow will disclose the proper reason; when he does, a storehouse of exciting information will have been unlocked.

In the bygone days, there was no Allegheny River. Instead, a glorified French Creek rose near the mouth of Clarion River, flowed upstream to Franklin, Pennsylvania, thence up modern French Creek, and emptied into Lake Erie somewhere near Erie, Pennsylvania. Salamanca, New York, lost a good bet by reason of this glacial action: before the ice came along, two good-sized rivers converged there, one from down around Warren (running backward up the present Allegheny valley) and the other being the present headwater of the Allegheny River in much its present shape. These streams converged at Salamanca and flowed off to Lake Erie, emptying in near Dunkirk, New York.

Many centuries of grinding ice changed the landscape somewhat: in the twinkling of an eye (geologically speaking) the Allegawe country was formed, the Allegheny River took shape, the Ohio River commenced emptying into the Mississippi. With this job done, the glacier went back home for some unknown reason, leaving a wealth of fine, sharp sand and rounded pebbles all over the regions north of the Ohio River. As a present-day reminder of this cataclysm, you or I may walk out on any towhead or island on the Allegheny River (or the upper Ohio River, for that matter) and pick up a piece of rose quartz, although the nearest known deposits are some 1,200 miles away. Not only rose quartz, mind you, but samples of an infinite variety of rock.

Gravel from the Allegheny and upper Ohio rivers is the most beautiful in all creation, and a fascinating pastime is to watch it rattle from a modern "sand digger," assorted in various sizes, wet and sparkling, all hues of the rainbow, trimmed with fascinating designs. If there wasn't such a wealth of it, these specimens would easily class as semiprecious stones. Another result, owing entirely to this glacial action, is that a person can walk barefoot (even if he has pink, tender toes) over any gravel bar on the Allegheny River with comparative ease, for each pebble is well-rounded and polished. A geologist can sit down in one spot on an Allegheny River towhead and find enough samples of various formations to fill a trunk—without any effort on his part other than reaching out to get them.

So, all in all, the glacier was a Good Thing. It is fortunate that it selected those ancient days for the job it had to do; otherwise the complexion of the events which happened since certainly would be another story. There seems no guarantee that this glacier does not recur in regular cycles; there may be another one someday. To date, nobody has been able to put his finger on the cause—so it is impossible to predict. A few fools wonder and shake their heads at the extravagance of the new 200-inch telescope, but who can tell? Maybe this remarkable instrument will disclose the answer to the glacial riddle! If Buffalo, New York, is to be buried under ten million tons of ice in the year 10,662, seems it would be worth knowing about—holders of perpetual leases on real estate might raise an inquisitive eyebrow, at any rate.

When our Frenchman-trapper friend Kinney stood on the shores of the Allegheny River at Olean, this glacier story was an old one. The Mound Builders had come and gone (perhaps a tribe before them) and the Allegawes had been shoved southward. Indian villages dotted the peaceful shores of a clear-flowing river at a dozen or more locations.

The year 1669 is interesting in Allegheny River history inasmuch as it marks the beginnings of white man's interest in the territory. Rather late in the shaping of American events as a whole, when you consider that New York City was so important that the English had stolen it from the Dutch several years before (not such a crime when you read how the Dutch came in possession of the place), and the existence of the Mississippi River had been known for some hundred and twenty years. Jamestown, Virginia, was still the seat of government, but within thirty years it was to be moved up to Williamsburg. Over in England an obscure poet named John Milton had just written *Paradise Lost* and considered himself lucky with a contract from his publisher which paid him about $25 down, and promises of perhaps $75 more at some obscure date in the future. But 1669 is important to our interests because that year a French geographer named René Robert Cavalier, Sieur de La Salle, barged off from Canada "to see the west."

You know, it is a wonder, as wonders go, how those pioneer fellows got around the country the way they did. Like as not a party of them would strike off into the tall timber with no idea on earth where they were heading, and then disappear from civilized society for months, and months, and months—then someday turn up again, usually with a big story to tell. Most of them were young bucks, and full of vinegar, and used excuses (for their wives mainly, I think) such as converting the heathen Indians, and then there

was always the possibility that they would discover the Pacific Ocean. There is no denying that the Pacific Ocean needed a good sound discovering in those days. A husband could look his wife plumb square in the eyes and say, "Honey, I've got a notion creeping around in my bones that the Pacific Ocean is over the mountains yonder, and down the river apiece."

And when his wife laid down the corn pone and fixed her mouth in a thin white line and narrowed those pools of limpid blue into meaningful slits and said, "What would *you* do with the Pacific Ocean if you had it right here in your lap, I ask you?"—and then he could muster up great convictions and visions and speak of the crying need for westward expansion, and shorter trade routes, and the good of the white man, and the progress of civilization. A grand and noble thought! Best of all, it generally went over.

La Salle may have come down the Allegheny River. There is an equal chance that he did not. At this late date nobody knows for certain. His exalted Keeper of the Diary lost the books or had them stolen from him, so there is no record. La Salle recounted his adventures to various persons afterwards, but they were listening to a lot of strange names and hearing of remote places, and didn't get the drift of what he was trying to tell them. Apparently La Salle never troubled to scribble any notes of his own. One thing certain, he was certainly not impressed with the Allegheny River if he did descend it. His head was full of Chinamen and Pacific Ocean. This disputed trip of his was in 1669. He did go down the Ohio River part way, but that is no concern of ours, and his connection with Allegheny River history is noticed here only because of the possibility and because every good history of the Allegheny River includes it. So Amen to Bob La Salle and a passing salute to his real explorations, which have nothing to do with the Allegheny. If he has any remote connection with our immediate business, it was when he planted a cross and column at, or near, the mouth of the Mississippi, on which were inscribed the name and arms of the French sovereign, taking possession in his name, of all lands watered by the river and its tributaries, on which he bestowed the name of Louisiana. This was in April, 1682. Five years later his crew murdered him for getting them all hopelessly lost, vainly looking for the mouth of the Mississippi.

After all these things, you will notice, the Allegheny River still is not officially discovered.

CHAPTER FIVE

LITTLE use of pretense any longer; one moment the valley of the Allegheny was loaded with stupidly dull Indians scratching meager plots of corn; in another wink of the eye, these same Indians were yipping and yelling, and stumbling and falling, and going on at a great rate—drunk—the lot of them. Whisky had arrived. Therefore the white race had arrived. The picture is a sorry one. An English mapmaker named Lewis Evans wrote an account of it; some historians raise the doubt as to whether Evans saw the things he tells about firsthand; I am sure I don't know

—nor do I know who does know (if anyone), but the urge to share this gossip with the Reader is overwhelmingly strong within me. Without wasting any more time about it, let us get to the matter:

"The English manner of carrying on the Indian trade is this: The regular Traders undertake twice or oftener each year journeys to the Indian villages, their Pack-horses laden with Strowds, match-coats, hats, looking-glasses, beads and braclets of glass, knives, and all manner of Gawdy Toys and Knacks for children, as well as guns, flints, Powder and Lead, and cags of potent Rum to be watered when they arrive in the Indian country. When there these Traders live with the Indians, selling them goods in prospect of the season's fur catch and often keeping one or more Squaws as wives and are trusted by their neighbours for they are content with a meer trifle of two or three hundred per centum profit above the cost of the Trade-goods and transport which it is said are nigh equal.

"Other Traders there are who frequently creep into the Woods with spiritous liquor and cheating trifles, after the Indian hunting camps, in the Winter season, and putting down severall Cags before them, make them drunk selling their liquor at ten times its value to the great injury of the Fair Trader who supplies them with all the conveniences for hunting; for as they will sell even their wearing shirt for inebriating liquors, they must be supplied anew in the Fall of the year by a Trader. These Traders are the most vicious and abandoned Wretches of our Nation and the

Indians hold them in great contempt as a set of Mean Dishonest mercenary Fellows and complain that they debauch their young women, and even their wives, when the husbands are from home or drunk. When your Indian has once got a smack of Rum he is never

sober for ten days or untill there is no more left. Days and nights are passed in jovial, Amorous topers and in convivial songs, dances, and sacrifices to Venus; for in these frolics both sexes take such liberties with each other, and act without constraint or shame such scenes as they would abhor when sober or in their senses. But, at last, the liquor running low, and being most of them sick through intoxication, they become more sober; and now the dejected, lifeless sots would pawn everything they own for a mouthful of spirits to settle their stomachs.

"This is the time for the Wenches to make their market; for at these riots, every fellow has his own quart of Rum, holding it by the neck; and with this, his beloved friend, he roves about continually, singing, roaring and reeling to and fro, presenting his bottle to every one, offering a drink; And is sure to meet his beloved Female whom he complacently begs to drink with him. She, being furnished with an empty Bottle, concealed in a mantle, at last consents and taking a good long draught, blushes, drops her pretty face on her bosom and artfully discharges the Rum into her Bottle. This she privately conveys to her secret store; and when the Comic Farce is over, the Wench retails this precious Cordial at her own price.

"The most considerable of the Traders of whom there are about one hundred and of the greatest respectability are these: Thomas McKee who has traded across the mountains since the Shawanese left Minisink, John Fraser who hath a Store-house and Gun-smithy at Venango, Paul Pierce who roves Westward to the Wabasha, Hugh Crawford, Edward Ward, James and Alexander Lowery, and Alexander Maginty who gave me an Account of the course of the Ohio, and William Trent and George Croghan who have lately been concerned together. This last is a Dublin Irishman who is a meer Idol among his countrymen, the Irish traders, and the Indians from whom he has taken a Squaw to wife, and is said to control one-fourth the Trade of

the Ohio Country and to have many servants and factors and associates and to have hundreds of Pack-horses for the hawling of his Trade-goods. He has Store-houses on Susquehanna fourteen days from the Ohio, at the Redstone, at the forks of the Ohio, at Logstown, at Pickawillani and among the Sandusky Indians seated on Lake Erie and elsewhere and it is said has made ventures down the Ohio to the Kantucqui River and the Wabasha. His most considerable Plantation in the Indian Country is at Pine Creek (the side of Etna) a league up the Allegeni where he has severall fields cleared and stockadoed, together with log-houses, batteaux and canoes, and a Factor in residence.

"I must not omit giving one caution to those in power. Hitherto we have apprehended no greater scheme of the French than making a Chain of Communication between Canada and the mouth of the Mississippi. As this was remote, we thought ourselves but little interested in it. Now they are about to attempt it nigher us on Ohio as is daily witnessed by the talk of the French traders in that country and by the late progress of the Sieur de Céloron down the Ohio and the planting of leaden plates in the name of the French king; if this succeed, it is not Ohio only must fall under their Dominion, but the country thence Southward to the Bay of Mexico. We charge the Indians with fickleness, but with greater propriety we should charge ourselves with great want of sense or experience, in supposing any Nation is to be tied to another, by any thing other than interest. 'Tis a custom, established with the English, to purchase the friendship of wavering Nations with many gifts, and to abandon their friends. Hence those who know this mixture of weakness and baseness that possesses us, keep members of Council in the French interest as well as ours, to keep us under a perpetual contribution. In consequence we are like to lose both our Trade and our Domains to the French who daily court the Indian Nations with subtle blandishments and sumptuous presents."

CHAPTER SIX

For well over two generations after La Salle's original passage through the Ohio regions, the Indian traders dispensed merchandise and rum at their old stands, and sent pack horses back east laden with furs —beautiful, select furs—to drape the fashionable female society of Boston, New York, Philadelphia, and Williamsburg. Business hummed along with alacrity, and grew, and prospered. English and French and Indian and half-breed rubbed shoulders and got along tolerably well, considering, largely because, for some eighty years, neither French nor English thought of creating any permanent town or settlement on the Allegheny or Ohio rivers.

Then, one fine day, the French foresaw A New Nation in the wilderness out there beyond the Allegheny Mountains, and considered it was high time to stake some claims. It took the English some little time to wake up. Who, after all, thought the English, would want a region described by their own official mapmaker, Lewis Evans, this way:

"In vermin the Ohio Country is surpassing abundant every rocky knoll bearing its Den of venemous

Reptiles; so much so that in flood the voyager durst set foot ashore. The stinging flies and divers other Insects but particularly Muskeetose in this country are like to rival the Seven Plagues of Egypt. . . ."

Who would want to settle in such a place?

The French did.

As well may be imagined, it takes some ingenuity to stake out a continent in a manner at once to attain shockproof title to it. More so when the territory already is inhabited by persons who feel they have some prior claims in the matter.

And so, one hot July day, 1749, a bedraggled group of Frenchmen appeared at Warren, Pennsylvania, without much advance notice. Warren was the site of a small Indian village called Chauougon those days. The Indians turned out en masse, and the Indian kids whooped and yelled and pointed, and the Indian dogs barked and carried on, for this was an unusual event: a regular glorified circus parade. Some twenty canoes loaded with palefaces bumped down out of the mouth of Conewango Creek. Twenty canoes bearing some 246 persons (so say the accounts which were written, I fear, by some dusty historian who never tried to load 246 persons in twenty canoes and bring them down Conewango Creek in the middle of a July drought) and among these strangers were soldiers, Canadian Indians, and at least one chaplain. This was an Event. This was an Expedition. This was M. Céloron de Bienville and party, all the way from Montreal and above.

Céloron not only had 246 persons in his canoes; he had a lot of baggage and provisions and stuff, and a batch of lead plates. These lead plates turned out to be the most interesting lead plates in all the world. You'll be surprised if you haven't already heard about them!

Without much ado, Céloron directed his canoe party to a landing on the south shore of the Allegheny River (which he termed La Belle Rivière, for the French did not distinguish between the Ohio and the Allegheny those days) near a fine big red oak tree which formed a prominent landmark, being situated in a strip of bottom land and plainly visible for some distance around. Here the French party disembarked, got out some shovels, and dug a hole near this red oak.

You may easily imagine that the Indians were "taking in" this show, and the guttural comment which passed between the braves at this gravedigging scene must have run something on this order:

Short Indian: "Somebody dead, maybe?"

Tall Indian: "Hole not big nuf wide for um bury man—maybe for um dog."

Shorty: "Um damn fools bury um dog in a hole? What for bury um dog in a hole? Throw 'im in river and let 'im float down."

Sky-jack: "Sure um bury dog; Paleface hide stuff and keep stuff; no good stuff he hide and he keep; see him priest have him rag? He blow nose on him rag and keep in him pocket. White man damn fool."

Shorty: "What him white man do with it?"

Sky-jack: "Look him, white man! Him bury not dog; him put hunk lead in him hole!"

Shorty: "Him medicine man make hocus-pocus on him hole and him hunk lead! Some spirit in him hunk lead, maybe, huh?"

Sky-jack: "You see here some son-bitch trick, I bet you. Frenchman no drag down here in hot summer to bury no damn lead plate for no good, I bet you."

Shorty: "Maybe he mean he bury lead like we bury hatchet—no make bullets with buried lead, maybe."

Sky-jack: "Frenchman never give big hunk lead to hole in ground for nothing, you bet you; him Frenchman save stuff too much."

Shorty: "So what? Him big French powwow over hunk lead don't hurt Brave Indian. Anyhow pretty soon him Frenchmens go downriver, never come back, maybe."

Sky-jack: "Look um! Paleface put um sign on tree with nail and hammer. Metal sign, him put um on tree."

Shorty: "Him paleface want remember him tree, maybe. Maybe forget him tree. Put sign on him tree. Tell him where is hole in ground and hunk lead."

Sky-jack: "Better you get Fleetfoot. Go downriver and tell um Indian villages look out! for lead plate stuff and French. Warn Indian fellows. Look out! Son-bitch business start around here plenty soon nuf, I bet you."

Now we come to a point in history which is

hard to interpret; in short, whether Céloron figured the Indians right or wrong. We don't know. Perhaps Céloron knew the Indians simply could not resist digging up that lead plate and giving it the once-over. Maybe he thought the ceremony would ward off such an occurrence, feeling the Indians would give the red oak tree and vicinity wide berth, by reason of the Scripture which had been read and the blessing which had been invoked. If Céloron imagined the lead plate was secure in its hole in the ground, he was an imbecile; if he intended it should be dug up, he was a genius.

An Indian, whatever else may be said of him, has the curiosity of a goose, same as you and I. Sky-jack or somebody of the red tribe unearthed that lead plate. Upon its face he found unintelligible jargon. French words filled the small 7½ by 11-inch slab to capacity. Interpreted, the wording read this way:

In the year 1749—the reign of Louis XV, King of France, we, Céloron, commandant of a detachment sent by Monsieur the Marquis of Gallisonnière, Commander in Chief of New France, to establish tranquillity in certain Indian villages of these cantons, have buried this plate at the confluence of the Ohio and of To Ra Da Koin, this 29th July, near the river Ohio, otherwise Beautiful River, as a monument of renewal of possessions, which we have taken of said river, and of all its tributaries, and of all the land on both sides, as far as to the sources of said rivers—inasmuch as the preceding Kings of France have enjoyed [this possession] and have maintained it by their arms and by treaties, especially by those of Ryswick, Utrecht, and Aix-la-Chapelle.

Well, the Indians had no interpreter, so they did the next best thing; they lugged it to somebody who could read it. This happened to be Sir William Johnson, English superintendent of Indian affairs. He informed the Indians that it involved possession of their lands, which the French were taking for themselves. Sky-jack was right.

Céloron, meanwhile, paddled his canoes on down the Allegheny. Below Franklin, Pennsylvania, he buried a second slab of lead with much the same fanfare as attended the Warren ceremony. He stopped in at an important Indian village at the mouth of Brokenstraw Creek and had a powwow, and expressed "surprise" upon seeing a cabin or building being erected for the convenience of English traders there. This sort of thing had been going on for a hundred years, but now the French were "surprised." Intelligent people act that way just before a war commences.

It is interesting to notice that Céloron did not plant a lead plate at the site of Pittsburgh, that important point where today the Monongahela and Allegheny rivers merge to form the Ohio River. The reason is explainable enough; for Céloron had no advance notice that the forks of those rivers was an important location; it didn't look important, surely. Low, boggy ground, and the air full of those "moskeetose." On down the Ohio River he deposited four more plates, the last of which was buried at the mouth of the Big Miami. Then, by a devious route, he and his party went home to Montreal.

It may be of interest, in passing, to notice that the plate which was buried at the mouth of the Muskingum River was found by some boys in swimming in 1798, and is today preserved, if I am correctly informed, by the Antiquarian Society of Massachusetts. Another plate, buried near the mouth of the Great Kanawha River, was located in 1846 at Point Pleasant, Virginia (now West Virginia, of course). The first plate buried at Warren, Pennsylvania, eventually came into the possession of Governor George Clinton of New York.

You boys who would seek buried treasure may get busy now: look sharply near the big Indian Rock some nine miles below Franklin, Pennsylvania. One of the missing plates is in that vicinity. Another lies somewhere down the Ohio River between Wheeling and Parkersburg. The last one, placed at the mouth of the Big Miami, hasn't shown up yet.

CHAPTER SEVEN

A STORY handed down from Indian days relates a rather curious scrap of animal lore. One day several Indian hunters found a rat somewhere along the Allegheny River valley. They killed it, and examined the rat with great curiosity, for none of the party had seen such an animal before. The limp rodent was taken to a wise old Indian chief. He squizzed up his eyes, recognized it, and deep furrows of a frown appeared above the wrinkled crow-tracks about his eyes. He made a pronouncement to this effect: "An animal like this one was found while our venerable grandfathers lived along the Delaware. It was found just before the white man came and took our hunting grounds there. It is an ill omen."

This rat story dates to the same period when Céloron and his party descended the Allegheny and the Ohio, planting their lead plates. Perhaps Mr. Rat was a Frenchman; perhaps he was an English stowaway. To the Allegheny Indians his arrival was a sign-of-the-times; as significant as the first low rumble of thunder on a sultry summer day from the vicinity of a westward hilltop; and the delicate, uneasy rustling of maple leaves in the dead calm before a thunderstorm. A common ordinary beady-eyed rat with a long, naked tail. Limp and dead. Filled with forebodings of strange portent.

Doubtless the ancient Indian chief who made this pronouncement looked up and down the sparkling blue waters of the Allegheny River that evening and saw the sun swallowed by a familiar hill, and watched with renewed keen eye as each tall pine was mirrored in blue and purple upon the glassy stillness of the river. He, in that olden time, was drinking deeply of a scene which he knew, deep in his heart, was ending. There was a bitter twist in that old pumping heart of his, and a catch in his throat.

Today there remains no timberland in the United States which has not, in some degree, become civilized—or marked by man in some form or another. Today we can have but faint conception of the primitive

Allegheny forest as it stood when the first rat appeared. Trees six to eight feet in diameter were not uncommon, and pines attaining 100 to 150 feet in height were everywhere, and as abundant as daisies in an abandoned pasture-field today. Oak, chestnut, beech; maple, hickory, walnut—not "fine examples" here and there, but everywhere, in abandon, filling ravines and hillsides, shutting off daylight and vision in all directions. These forest lands were carpeted with dead and decaying logs fallen in confusion, intertwined with vines and shrubs, making impassable barriers to ingress of animal and human being alike. Woe be to the deer or elk which, in some frenzy of fright, plunged into such a labyrinth to be snared and snagged by rugged vegetation, bound fast by thongs of vine, and left to die after vain strugglings from which there was no release. The Indian traveled by water where possible, and only upon beaten trails otherwise; his villages were made on the banks of streams where natural meadows existed. No human talked of "conquering nature" those days; at best it was a niggardly compromise.

Timber, timber, timber! Large glades, or natural meadows, known to be common in parts of the wilderness elsewhere, were not frequent in the primitive Allegheny forest country. Here, in this wooded watershed, stood forest giants which were to become joists in houses of Cincinnati, Louisville, Natchez, and New Orleans; here in the silent reaches of "tall sticks" were the plankings which would barge coal—millions and millions of tons of coal—down the Ohio and Mississippi rivers;

yes, here were the sidewalk plankings for Creole towns in the South; masts for ships to sail the briny deep—the Allegheny valley was to become the lumberyard of the nation in a day of westward expansion, and before the forests of Michigan, Wisconsin, and Minnesota were exploited.

The sons of the old Indian chief who beheld the rat were to know the peculiar, studied chunk! of a woodsman's ax, and their sons and their sons' sons were to become familiar with rough, heavy, cumbersome pine boards and know the peculiar clap! as board is dropped upon board with its cushioning effect. Oh! these sons would know: they would see dew on the grass, fog in the air, early spring, clear water in the rivers, small bubbles of white froth—they would also know a new pungent smell in the morning air, the light-blue smoke of a steam sawmill boiler, the whine of a circular saw, and the miracle of sized planking from the heart of a tall tree.

A small rat with a naked tail presaged white man's domination in the Allegheny valley, it is told. Wise little rat!—and foolish, too, for his beady eyes and quizzical nose apparently did not tell him the difference between a Frenchman and an Englishman. Very likely he came with the former, but soon found himself under the floors of the latter. Not that a rat would care about *that;* but it does seem to me, if I were a rat with a voracious appetite, methinks I would trade with the English every time: crumbs would be more generous.

CHAPTER EIGHT

THAT ROVING peripatetic, George Washington, got himself introduced to Allegheny River water in dramatic fashion. Washington fought no battles in the Allegheny country, nor did he acquire properties in the region that we know about, so there is little use meddling with the truth or trying to stretch him into our story in the light of a hero. The plain and simple statement of the matter seems to be that Washington was the first known person to distinguish himself by falling into the Allegheny River. He made an extremely clumsy job of it, and the only triumphant note in the whole affair seems to be how he lived to tell the tale!

Major Washington was twenty-one years old when this event happened—but first we must explore the reasons why he was obliged to cross the Allegheny on a bleak December night in 1753. Shortly after Céloron planted his lead plates, the French took definite steps to press their claim of ownership of the Allegheny valley. Forts were established at the headwaters of French Creek and at Venango (the present location of Franklin). English traders were driven out of the country, and those who refused to go were arrested and taken to Canada for jailing purposes. This change-around was made in typically blunt military fashion; for instance, the French dispossessed John Frazier of his buildings and belongings at Venango and appropriated the lodgings to themselves; this Frazier, who was an English gunsmith, was told to git! and git quick! as were all others of his nationality. Frazier dropped down the Allegheny and located himself near the mouth of Turtle Creek on the Monongahela. Temporarily, at least, he was safe there. To say he was "burned up" over this piracy of his belongings is to put the matter mildly—but what else could he do?

Sometimes retribution comes swiftly in this world. Frazier was puttering around his cabin one day when two travelers hove up on his premises, down there at Turtle Creek. One of them he knew to be Christopher Gist, a famed guide of the region; the other he certainly had heard about, Major George Washington. The major was interested in some vast real estate dealings down along the Ohio River and these French seizures had not done his belongings any good, to say the least. Now the major was armed with a letter from the governor of Virginia addressed to the commander of the French forces asking them, oh, so politely, to remove themselves and go back to Canada where they belonged. John Frazier's eyes brightened at the receipt of this intelligence, and he welcomed these two travelers to his cabin with a hearty "What can I do for you, boys?"

Frazier was chock-full of reliable information

about the state of affairs up the Allegheny and this, coupled with his long association with the topography of the region, made what he had to say to Washington and Gist quite important. The plan of procedure was outlined in the cabin at Turtle Creek. Winter was threatening (for this was in November, 1753) and Washington, wishing to expedite his mission, could thank his lucky stars for having visited gunsmith Frazier.

To make a long story short (which is a shame, for it was an interesting journey), Washington and Gist delivered their letter, got little or no satisfaction from anybody, and made haste for home. The return trip was spurred by the cold weather, and also because the Indians in the Allegheny valley had turned their sympathies toward the French and, as a consequence, the business of plodding along in wild woodlands was not exactly a healthy occupation for two lone Englishmen. An Indian guide already had turned traitor, and had tried to pot-shot the two of them from behind a tree. The tracks our two emissaries were making in the snow as they headed from Venango toward Frazier's cabin on Turtle Creek were—well, they were not merely man tracks; they were man-in-a-hurry tracks—widely spaced, and no fooling about them.

The route Washington and Gist took necessitated crossing the Allegheny River in the vicinity of Pittsburgh. Near as we can tell at this late date they must have come down Guyosuta Creek, which "dreens" into the Allegheny back of Six Mile Island—about where

Lock Number 2 is located today, above Etna, Pennsylvania. The cold weather had produced a lot of shore ice, which extended out about fifty yards from each shore, and the main channel was well filled with slush ice, which was "making" with alarming rapidity. This obstacle confronted our travelers one evening about nightfall. There was nothing they could do about it in the dark, so they camped along the shore and waited for daybreak.

It is easy to set these things down on paper while comfortably seated in a warm room, and this author wishes to go on record that he would not have traded places with those two gentlemen for love or money. Consider a moment! Here were two "hikers" with no equipment other than knapsacks and some sort of 1753 Boy Scout hatchet. Treacherous shore ice, freezing weather, and the channel of the Allegheny loaded with those thick steel-blue cakes of "fresh-made" ice such as the Allegheny alone can produce. Problem: get across without getting wet.

The way Washington and Gist looked at it, a raft was the only solution, and so, I suppose, it was. Washington took his little hatchet in hand soon as day commenced to show and started a campaign on tree-chopping. Doubtless they selected dead trees, and drift, and stuff such as that to work on, inasmuch as dead timber is much lighter and more likely to float when tied into a river raft. Anyhow it was a long-drawn-out task, and by nightfall, after a complete day of hacking and hauling, the raft was as finished as it ever was going to be. Now, it is a trait of young men to want immediately to try out something they have just sweat over for any length of time, and Washington and Gist were no exception: they eyed their raft with some satisfaction and determined to cross the Allegheny that very night aboard it.

Mark what happens now with special care, for this is Lesson Number One of what not to do on a raft when there is running ice in the Allegheny River. In order to propel the raft across the river, these fellows equipped themselves with a couple of pushing poles, stout enough to lean some weight on and long enough to touch bottom all the way across. They got the raft successfully launched off the edge of the shore ice and picked up their poles and commenced "setting" over the river fast as they could go. This sort of technique is all well and good when there is no floating ice to hinder, but Rule Number One of moving any frail object through heavy ice running in a current is to drift with the ice, and compromise with it, and play with it, and treat it with all respect, and forge toward the far shore only when it will let you do so—even if you drift downstream as far as the Gulf of Mexico.

In their anxiety to get across the Allegheny, Washington and Gist apparently neglected these simple precautions and suddenly were startled to see a huge block of ice bear down on the raft with the very evident intention of swallowing it. This is what comes of not taking care; it can happen no other way. Washington tried to stop the raft by jamming his pole down and leaning on it with all his might. Allegheny ice won't stop for anybody short of God Almighty, let alone George Washington, and it is not in the least surprising to learn that the oncoming ice cake took George in tow, and the raft, and the pole, and all, and quicker than it takes to tell, Major Washington was in the water (ten feet deep, by the way) and grabbing for raft logs. This event would have been funny if the water had not been so cold.

By some hook or crook the raft skirted the shore of Six Mile Island and the two navigators escaped to terra-firma with their job half-done (for they were in the middle of the river now) and night had closed down for certain. The raft was gone. Washington was wet. The thermometer was flirting with the zero mark. If this author ever meets George Washington in the Hereafter, and has the rare privilege of an audience with him, the first question shall be a demand for a full account of how that night on Six Mile Island was spent —yes, to the total exclusion of all else the Father of our Country did in his fabulous lifetime, that—and that alone—stands out as the most miraculous eight or ten hours of his career. Did you ever see anybody dragged out of the river in winter? Even five minutes' exposure is sufficient to sap all the vitality from an ordinary mortal, and leave him blue and numb and chilled to the bone. I saw a man dragged out one night—he fell in with an overcoat on—and when he was brought ashore the rescuers took off the overcoat and stood it on the ground like a tin tent—with the sleeves standing out rigid as tree limbs! As for the late occupant, he looked like a white cigar-store Indian, just as stiff, just as stolid, and just as dead. What's more, he had been full of whisky before he fell in! Another time I saw . . . but that is off the track.

Washington survived that night on Six Mile Island somehow, and it was his partner Christopher Gist who got his hands and feet frozen. If you have any doubts about it being cold that night, in the morning the main channel of the river was frozen over solid and these two lucky fellows walked ashore! The light-blue wood smoke tumbling from the chimney at Frazier's cabin must surely have looked good to Washington and Gist that evening.

This now is story enough of George Washington's exploits in the valley of the Allegheny: a fruitless journey and a good ducking.

Sometime in the late 1830's two men did crack up a raft at Jemison on the upper Allegheny on a February evening, had a narrow escape getting to an island. The snow was two feet deep, the weather intensely cold, they had no tinder. Marooned there and aware they would shortly freeze to death unless extreme measures were immediately taken, they resorted to a prolonged wrestling match. Betweentimes they shouted for help. Then they wrestled some more. Concluding that this course would result in nothing better than physical exhaustion, they explored the island, discovered some wood slabs. With these they constructed a small raft, got aboard, and floated down the stream several miles. By lucky chance they happened on a campfire, discovered a hunter "holed in" for the night, and managed to push ashore. "This escape," says the original author of the incident, "is only one of a thousand true tales which might be told of peril and suffering on this river."

Plenty of surprises were in store for everybody along the Allegheny River in the spring of 1754, even before the dogwood and trilliums were in bloom. The French, under M. Contrecœur, captain of one of the companies of the Detachment of the French Marine, commander-in-chief of his Most Christian Majesty's troops, now on the Beautiful River, came down the Allegheny from Venango (Franklin, Pennsylvania) to the "forks" where the Allegheny and Monongahela join to form the Ohio, with one thousand men (Indians and Frenchmen) and eighteen cannons. This early-spring excursion required sixty batteaux and three hundred canoes. Never, before or since, have the waters of the Allegheny River borne so large a group of humanity, operating as a single unit.

But it is extremely dangerous to say "never" when writing history, inasmuch as "never" is a long period and covers a deal of space and time. Right this minute, even as the ink of the paragraph above is still wet, the author wishes to refute the statement he made! Parties of persons exceeding threefold Contrecœur's have landed hundreds of times on the banks of the Allegheny River at Pittsburgh exactly where this French party landed. The author knows this to be a fact, for he landed a good many of these parties himself, he being pilot on an enormous sidewheel excursion boat which made a business of disgorging humanity—whole populations of humanity—on the banks of the Allegheny River; not Indians and French, it is true, but a polyglot lot at that: our captain frequently remarked that, if the boat were to sink with an excursion of Pittsburghers aboard, with all the nationalities represented, the customers would be hollering for help in thirty languages. Just the same, coming back to the French expedition, Contrecœur brought down the biggest Allegheny River excursion on record inasmuch as he commenced at Franklin, Pennsylvania, some 126 miles above Pittsburgh, and was on the Allegheny for the whole of his journey, while the latter-day excursion boat piloted by the author "wore out" her trips on the Ohio River and merely entered the mouth of the Allegheny to rid herself of her crowds.

Apparently this big French and Indian party had little or no navigation difficulty, and paddled out of the Allegheny successfully enough, for on the 17th of April, 1754, they arrived at Pittsburgh intact. Of course, literally, they did not arrive at Pittsburgh; they arrived at the spot where Pittsburgh was to be someday; they thought they were arriving at a barren, forsaken, marshy, mosquito-infested location which would be a strategic site for a French fort, and they intended to locate there. What Contrecœur did not intend, and what he did find, was a group of Englishmen already on the grounds equipped with some hammers, and saws, and hatchets, and baggage and stuff, fixing to build an English fort.

Contrecœur shooed the English away merely by engaging in some Loud Talk, a task that was relatively easy inasmuch as there were but few English and many French. Loud Talk, as a general rule, comes to nothing, but in this case Contrecœur started a grand-and-glorious war between England and France, which was to reach into Europe, Asia, and Africa. Would you care to hear what he said? There certainly is no objection to setting the Loud Talk down in black-and-white, because it is polite enough to keep company with the Bible. Hear it, then:

"Nothing can surprise me more than to see you attempt a settlement upon the lands of the King, my master, which obliges me now, Sir, to send you this gentleman, Chevalier Le Mercier, Captain of the Artillery of Canada, to know of you, Sir, by virtue of what authority you are come to fortify yourself within the dominions of the King, my master. The action seems so contrary to the last Treaty of Peace, at Aix La Chapelle, between his Most Christian Majesty and the King of Great Britain, that I do not know to whom to impute such an usurpation, as it is incontestable that the lands situated along the Beautiful River belong to his Most Christian Majesty."

The full text of this froth reels along for several more paragraphs and finally demands a "precise answer."

This verbal exchange, and the occupation of the

lands at the mouth of the Allegheny by the French, was the commencement of the old French and Indian War and, more broadly, the Seven Years' War.

The site of Pittsburgh became Fort Duquesne now, and while the French tenanted the property a shocking affair occurred there on the bank of the Allegheny River. The next chapter very well may be entitled, "Something Which Polite History Books Generally Omit." I daresay most Pittsburghers, hurrying to and fro on the many bridges, and ramps, and crowded streets of today have no idea—at least but a remote idea—that such things could have happened anywhere east of the "wild and woolly West" let alone in their own front yards! And happened so recently that there may be old mud turtles still living which witnessed the gruesome scene!

CHAPTER NINE

THE SPRING following the erection of Fort Duquesne an eighteen-year-old youth, named James Smith, accompanied a party of three hundred men from the frontiers of Pennsylvania, for the purpose of opening a road over the mountains.

This was an English expedition, and the road was designed to allow passage of troops and cannon into the regions of Fort Duquesne. For the English, under General Braddock, meant to march over this mountain road and drive the French back to Canada.

When within a few miles of Bedford Springs, James Smith was sent to the rear to hasten the progress of some wagons loaded with provisions and stores for the use of the woodcutters. Having delivered his orders, he was returning, in company with another young man, when they were suddenly fired upon by a party of three Indians from a cedar thicket which skirted the road. Smith's companion was killed upon the spot; and although he himself was unhurt, yet his horse was so much frightened by the flash and report of the guns as to become totally unmanageable, and after a few plunges threw him with violence to the ground. Before he could recover his feet, the Indians sprang upon him and, overpowering his resistance, secured him as prisoner. One of them demanded, in broken English, whether "more white men were coming up," and upon his answering them in the negative, he was seized by each arm and compelled to run with great rapidity over the mountain until night, when the small party encamped and cooked their suppers. An equal share of their scanty provision was given to the prisoner, and in other respects, although strictly guarded, he was treated with great kindness.

On the evening of the second day, after a rapid walk of fifty miles through cedar thickets, and over very rocky ground, they reached the western side of Laurel Mountain and beheld, at a little distance, the smoke of an Indian encampment.

His captors now fired their guns and raised the scalp halloo! This is a long yell for every scalp that has been taken, followed by a rapid succession of shrill, quick, piercing shrieks—shrieks somewhat resembling laughter in the most excited tones.

They were answered from the Indian camp below by a discharge of rifles, and a long whoop, followed by shrill cries of joy, and all thronged out to meet the party. Smith expected instant death at their hands, as they crowded around him; but, to his surprise, no one offered him any violence. They belonged to another tribe, and entertained the party in the camp with great hospitality, respecting the prisoner as the property of their guests.

On the following morning Smith's captors continued their march, and on the evening of the next day arrived at Fort Duquesne. When within half a mile of the fort they again raised the scalp halloo, and fired their guns as before. Instantly the whole garrison was in commotion. Cannons were fired, drums were beaten, and the French and Indians ran out in great numbers to meet the party and partake of their triumph.

Smith was again surrounded by a multitude of savages, painted in various colors, and shouting with delight; but their demeanor was by no means as pacific as that of the last party he had encountered. They rapidly formed in two lines, and brandishing their hatchets, ramrods, switches, called aloud for him to run the gantlet.

Never having heard of this Indian ceremony, he stood amazed for some time, not knowing what to do; but one of his captors explained to him that he was to run between the two lines and receive a blow from each Indian as he passed, concluding his explanation by exhorting him to "run his best" as the faster he ran the sooner the affair would be over.

The truth was very plain—and young Smith entered upon his race with great spirit. He was switched very handsomely along the lines for about three-fourths the distance, stripes only acting as a spur to greater exertions, and he had almost reached the extremity of the line, when a tall chief struck him a furious blow with a club upon the back of the head, and felled him to the ground.

Recovering himself in a moment, he sprang to his feet and started forward again, when a handful of sand was thrown in his eyes, which, in addition to the great pain, completely blinded him. He still attempted to grope his way through, but was again knocked down and beaten with merciless severity. He soon became insensible under such barbarous treatment, and recollected nothing more until he found himself in the hospital of the fort, under the hands of a French surgeon, beaten to a jelly, and unable to move a limb.

Here he was quickly visited by one of his captors —the same one who had given him such good advice when about to commence his race. He now inquired with some interest, if he felt "very sore." Young Smith replied that he had been bruised almost to death, and asked what he had done to merit such barbarity. The Indian replied that he had done nothing, but that it was the customary greeting of the Indians to their prisoners—that it was something like the English "how d'ye do," and that now all ceremony would be laid aside, and he would be treated with kindness.

Smith inquired if they had any news of General Braddock. The Indian replied that their scouts saw him every day from the mountains—that he was advancing in close columns through the woods (this he indicated by placing a number of red sticks parallel to each other, and pressed close together)—and that the Indians would be able to shoot them down "like pigeons."

James Smith rapidly recovered, and was soon able to walk upon the battlements of the fort, with the aid of a stick. While engaged in this exercise, on the morning of the 9th ——, he observed an unusual bustle in the fort. The Indians stood in crowds at the great gate, armed and painted. Many barrels of powder, balls, flints, were brought out to them, from which each warrior helped himself to such articles as he required. They were soon joined by a small detachment of French regulars; then the whole party marched off together.

Smith had a full view of this "army" as it passed, and was confident that there were not over four hundred men in all. He learned that it was detached against Braddock, who was now within a few miles of the fort; but from their great inferiority in numbers, he regarded their destruction as certain, and looked joyfully to the arrival of Braddock in the evening.

In the afternoon, however, an Indian runner arrived with far different intelligence. The battle had not yet ended when he left the field; but he announced that the English had been surrounded, and were shot down in heaps by an invisible enemy; that instead of flying at once or rushing upon their concealed foes, they appeared completely bewildered, huddled together in the center of the ring, and before sundown there would not be a man of them alive.

This intelligence fell like a thunderbolt upon Smith, who now saw himself irretrievably in the power of the savages, and could look forward to nothing but torture or endless captivity. He waited anxiously for further intelligence, still hoping that the fortune of the day might change.

But about sunset, he heard at a distance the well-known scalp halloo, followed by wild, quick, joyful shrieks, and accompanied by long-continued firing.

At dusk, the party returned to the fort, driving before them twelve British regulars, stripped naked, and

with their faces painted black, an evidence that the unhappy wretches were devoted to death. Next came the Indians, displaying their bloody scalps, of which they had immense numbers, and dressed in the scarlet coats, sashes, and military hats of the officers and soldiers. Behind all came a train of baggage horses, laden with piles of scalps, canteens, and all the accouterments of British soldiers.

The savages appeared frantic with joy, and when

Smith beheld them entering the fort, dancing, yelling, brandishing their red tomahawks, and waving their scalps in the air, while the great guns of the fort replied to the incessant discharge of the rifles without, he says that it looked as if hell had given a holiday and turned loose its inhabitants upon the upper world.

The most melancholy spectacle was the band of prisoners. They appeared dejected and anxious. Poor fellows! They had but a few months before left London, at the command of their superiors, and we may easily imagine their feelings at the strange and dreadful spectacle around them.

The yells of delight and congratulation were scarcely over when those of vengeance began. The prisoners (British regulars) were led out from the fort to the banks of the Allegheny, and to the eternal disgrace of the French commandant, were there burnt to death, with the most awful tortures. Smith stood upon the battlements and witnessed the shocking spectacle.

One at a time, each prisoner was tied to a stake, with his hands raised above his head, naked as the day he was born, and surrounded by Indians. They would touch him with red-hot irons, and stick his body full of pine splinters, and set them on fire—drowning the shrieks of the victim in yells of delight as they danced around him. As fast as one prisoner died under his tortures, another filled his place, until all perished. All this took place so near the fort that every scream of the victims must have rung in the ears of the French commandant!

Two or three days after this horrible spectacle, most of the Indian tribes dispersed and returned to their homes, as is usual with them after a great and decisive battle. Young Smith was claimed by his original captors and taken away by the tribe to which they belonged. He had many further adventures but lived to become a resident of Kentucky and later was held in high esteem and elected a member of the legislature.

These things happened upon the banks of the Allegheny River at Pittsburgh. No mark, no stone, no hint, no sign today—a bare cobblestone levee and some talk of building a concrete boulevard along Duquesne Way. Twelve Englishmen were roasted alive. Human grease in the soil caused a bare spot on the banks of the Allegheny where no grass would grow for a time.

Duquesne Way? That is where the excursion boat lands today. Lighthearted merrymakers shod in toeless slippers and polished oxfords come over the riverbanks there today.

No mark, no stone, no hint, no sign—

CHAPTER TEN

YOU WOULD THINK that the Allegheny River would get down to brass tacks now, and carry a burden of French commerce upon its bosom, and become La Belle Rivière of a New Nation. Doubtless the French military authorities considered they had "captured" the territory, and "occupied" it, and "seized" it, and "conquered" it. For a fact they had done all these things, and more: they had exterminated the English under General Braddock—utterly wiped an army off the face of the map and had laid Braddock in his grave for good measure—and they had allied the Indians to their cause. No Englishman was safe west of the Susquehanna River, and Indian raids caused terror among settlers up and down the Shenandoah valley. The English inhabitants of Winchester, Virginia, did not sleep soundly at night. If ever there was an open-and-shut case, it was this one: the valleys of the Allegheny, Ohio, and Mississippi rivers belonged to the French, along with all their "dreenings." Belonged with capital letters; they BELONGED to the French.

Of course, at this late date we know there was a mistake in these reckonings somewhere because little boys who were playing marbles in the streets of Boston while these things were going on were to shoulder muskets and help drive off the bloody English; they were to do this before the hair on their chests had fully grown in. These Boston boys were a strange breed called "Americans" and they, still with a soft down on their upper lips, were taught to believe the French were their friends.

Without posing as a wise philosopher, it would seem that the French military authorities made their Great Mistake in discounting that slow, awful, relentless, stubborn disposition which characterizes the English as a nation. Somebody should have told the French that the English wanted the Allegheny, the Ohio, and the Mississippi. And when the English people want something, the want is not confined to a group of military strategists who command English military forces; that want is as wide, and as broad, and as long as the English dominions. Every Englishman has a portion of that want tucked away inside his system somewhere. There is no stopping a want of this sort. Barely three years after twelve Englishmen had been burnt at the stake at Fort Duquesne, there came a superarmy of Englishmen over the Allegheny Mountains. There ensued no battle. The French exit is one of the most hasty on record. Fort Duquesne became Fort Pitt.

The main reason the Americans won the War of Independence in 1776 is because they were Englishmen in the first place—Englishmen hardened and toughened to primitive existence and fighting. The English Fort

Pitt became the American settlement of Pittsburgh. (To be exact, the town didn't officially have the H on the end for a good while; mostly it was spelled simply Pittsburg.

The Allegheny River rippled along very much unchanged all this while. If you had flown over it in an airplane in 1776 you wouldn't have known whether it was occupied by Indians or French or English or Americans. The forest-clad hills were intact, and everything was just about as the glacier left it. Oh, it is possible you might have spied out a village or so from the vantage point of an airplane, but that is about all. The chief difference was that rats and honeybees had intruded upon the countryside—and no aviator could observe these things. Honeybees were unknown to the Indian before the white man came; funny thing, that.

And so we have used up ten chapters getting the valley of the Allegheny loaded with Americans, honeybees, and rats. Slow progress, surely, but an exciting combination on any man's river.

CHAPTER ELEVEN

My great-grandmother Way arrived in Pittsburgh one April day of 1797 riding a cow, so she used to say. There is definite chance that she remembered the incident, although she was but three years old when this event took place. Perhaps her family impressed the story on her mind later on: nevertheless, it is true that William Anderson and his wife, with their brood of seven children, migrated from Carlisle, Pennsylvania, to Pittsburgh by crossing the Allegheny Mountains on a leisurely journey which required three years, and, unintentionally enough, they settled in the small village at the forks of the Ohio River—although the original intention of the migration was to forge on to Mercer, Pennsylvania, a small settlement some sixty miles northwest of Pittsburgh.

William Anderson was an Irish contractor and builder. On the way over the mountains he had erected courthouses at Bedford and Carlisle. His skill and experience in the erection of large buildings brought him in touch, at Pittsburgh, with Colonel James O'Hara, a kindred Irishman of Presbyterian faith who had roomy ideas and a need of many builders. Colonel

O'Hara put William Anderson to work building a glass plant: William Anderson housed his family at the corner of Penn and Fifth streets, where Horne's Department Store now stands, and kept them there from 1797 until 1811. To Mercer then? Far from it! William Anderson built a large and (for those times) palatial house at the corner of Penn and Eighth streets, and moved his family into it.

The Anderson children were well grown up in 1811 when this moving day took place: baby Clarissa was fifteen; Sarah, the oldest daughter, was twenty-nine, married and had two children; Paul was twenty-seven, tall and handsome, and considered a good catch, except that he had a good bit of his father's blarney about him; Mary Ann (who became my great-grandmother) was seventeen, and having the time of her young life. Mrs. Anderson had forgotten all about Mercer temporarily: she had settled down to the task of marrying off her daughters and acting as hostess to her husband's business associates, and entertaining the Presbyterian church elders at an occasional dinner.

The logical excuse for the intrusion of these family matters into this chapter is this: Mary Ann Anderson married my great-grandfather Abishai Way, and she lived to a ripe old age, and had a brilliant memory. Her son John, my grandfather, did what many a son does not do: he wrote down the stories of early Pittsburgh as his mother recited them, and kept these recordings in a large leather notebook. Of late years this very same notebook has been handed down through the Way family with the same ceremony which attends the conveyance of the Family Bible from one generation to the next. The author invites his reader to pull up his chair by the family hearth and listen to Mary Ann Anderson's gentle voice as she tells her recollections of early Pittsburgh. She is seated in a black rocking chair with a high back, which came over the mountains, and as she gently rocks and talks she occupies her hands with some crocheting she is engaged upon. Occasionally her glance goes beyond the room we are seated in, and strays out the window to her left, and rests lovingly on a helter-skelter "wild flower garden," the treasure of her outdoor world. Nobody is allowed to tend that garden; it tends itself; and itchweed, jimson, and dock are having a heyday among the trillium, bloodroot, and arbutus.

"No, there was no Presbyterian Church in Pittsburgh when our family arrived in 1797; nor was there a minister. The little city contained a hoodlum element who made it their business to make any preacher's life a continual torment. These fellows were mostly rivermen, used to a rough and hardy existence. They navigated flatboats from Pittsburgh to southern ports and had wonderful stomachs which would hold prodigious amounts of whiskey and rum. It was no infrequent rumor that most of these navigators never wore a stitch of clothes in summer from the time they left the 'Point' until they came back—this a mere sample of their disregard for society. Anyhow, Major Isaac Craig, Colonel O'Hara, Major Irwin, and a Major Denny got their heads together with Father and concluded to build a church—a log building—and call for a minister.

"This minister arrived fresh from Ireland in 1799 and created no little flutter among we Andersons: he was tall, slender, and wore black satin breeches, silk stockings, knee-buckles and pumps. His name was Robert Steele, and he came with his wife and child. His exit from Ireland had been of a hurried nature, and he neglected to bring his other four children with him. He accounted for this omission to Father by explaining, 'They told me I'd have my head cut off if I lingered another moment!'

"This primitive church, on Wood Street, had benches for pews. During one of the first services a young woman from Washington County arose in the middle of a sermon and let out a whoop! which could be heard for blocks, and straightway fell to the floor and set up a terrible moaning. Major Denny said she had an attack of the falling sickness, then prevalent in western Pennsylvania, and peremptorily ordered her out. With the assistance of 'Harris, the bell ringer' they toted her out to the side yard and threw water upon her with signal success.

"The very next week a pew collapsed and let Mother fall to the floor with a terrific crash. When she had been gathered up and reseated, Mrs. O'Hara leaned forward and whispered, 'Why, Mrs. Anderson, you are the last person I would have thought would have made a disturbance in church!'

"Mr. Steele was a free-mason and chaplain of a

lodge, the meetings of which were held in the second story of a house on the corner of Diamond Street (where Joseph Fleming's drugstore was in the 70's). He received $450 a year for his preaching services at the Presbyterian Church, and later this was raised to $600. He then sent for his other children in Ireland and had them brought to Pittsburgh by a friend of his, John Caldwell. When Caldwell arrived with the rest of the brood, Mother had a dinner for the lot of them, at which young John Caldwell distinguished himself by eating corn on the cob, cob and all. This brought muffled laughter from everyone save my sister Letitia, who was vexed with the rest of us, and upheld the embarrassed Irishman. She afterwards married him.

"On one occasion Reverend Mr. Reed, principal of a boys' school in Huntingdon, Pa., came over to Pittsburgh to attend Synod, and was a guest at our house. He met Mr. Steele, and accepted an offer to preach the Sunday sermon at the little log church. Mr. Steele was quite pleased, and on this particular Sabbath he hurried to church, grabbing up what he thought was a Hymn Book (scarce articles those days—only one copy in the whole church) and when he arrived at the church he handed it up to Reverend Mr. Reed, who occupied the pulpit. Mr. Steele sat down immediately below him and the service was opened. Reverend Mr. Reed opened the book to give out a hymn, and when his eyes fell on the pages, his brow took on a puzzled attitude. He leaned over the pulpit and said to Mr. Steele: 'Is this the kind of psawms ye sing here?'

The book happened to be a copy of Scott's Lessons, a popular school book of the day, and the Reverend Mr. Reed had opened it to John Gilpin.

"The Steele family lived in some upstairs rooms at the old Pittsburgh Academy on the corner of Cherry Alley and Third Street. Mother went over to see how the family fitted in their small quarters and when she got home Father asked her what she had found. 'Well, one thing I noticed, they must be very poor!' Mother exclaimed, and the next day some chickens were killed and dressed and I directed our hired boy, who carried the basket containing these things, to where the preacher and his family lived, and delivered the present.

"As times grew better for Preacher Steele, his wife was enabled to keep a servant, one Catherine O'Hara, who, by the way, was a relative of Colonel O'Hara. One day Mrs. Steele and Catherine quarreled about something or other and when Mr. Steele heard of it he went to the kitchen to reprove Catherine. She retorted by pushing him behind the door and would have proceeded further had not Catherine's mother unexpectedly appeared and rescued the minister, with the exclamation, 'You hussy! Would ye bate the priest?!'

"The little log church shortly became too small for the congregation and a subscription was taken to build a brick edifice. The money raised was far short of the actual costs of construction, so a lottery was proposed and many tickets sold. Father sold tickets to all his workmen, and the other elders did likewise. He gave one of these tickets to me, and it drew a six-dollar prize. A Mr. James Thompson drew $100 for a prize. The lottery wheel was in Squire Wilkins' office on Wood Street, corner of Fourth—he had a big place in Pittsburgh—his garden ran from the house up Wood to Diamond Street, and thence to Diamond Square. When the drawing was made, Mr. Steele's two eldest sons turned the wheel.

"William (afterwards Judge) Wilkins took quite an interest in the project, but somehow it was not a success. Somebody, I don't know who, was said to have drawn a prize of $1,000.

"Elizah Troville and old Mr. Goudy were the bricklayers at the new church. The new house was built around the old one, and over it. Troville, who used to be somewhat of a wag, told the country people that, when the walls were up, the old church was to be burned out of the way; and actually appointed a day for some of them to come to town and see the sight.

"The pulpit of the new church was a round, large box, rather high up. It was always a mystery to we children how the minister got into it—the steps, or stairs, were in someway concealed behind the pulpit. It was a grand church! The communion table was placed across the house in front of the pulpit; it was a long table with benches—there were silver goblets and nice, white table linen. Mr. James Cooper was one of the elders, and his daughter Peggy Davis always took care of the communion. The pews in the new church were arranged in the same pattern as in the original structure, so that each family had relatively the same locality—the new brick building, however, faced Wood Street, which was something different—as the old structure faced Virgin Alley.

"The Steele family now bought a lot from Colonel O'Hara and built themselves a brick house, with the help of Father, who had his workmen each give the preacher a day's work, gratis. Preacher Steele was an industrious fellow, and ready to turn a hand at anything that was required. On one occasion he told Father he had been hard at work all day. 'Yes,' he added, 'on something that anybody might worship and not break the commandment.' It was a bake oven which, by reason of his deficient education in that direction, had assumed an unusual and extraordinary shape. Mr. Steele always kept a fine garden.

"One winter morning about four o'clock a fire broke out and consumed a row of cheap frame houses and one brick on Wood Street above Sixth. The weather was intensely cold. Water was carried from the river in buckets, cutting through the ice to get it. Mr. Steele was at the fire, worked hard, got wet, and in nine days died.

"The free-masons raised $800 for Mrs. Steele. She lived on Seventh Street for some years and then removed to Colonel O'Hara's old log house (corner of Penn and Pitt Streets) in the King's Orchard. Mrs. Steele was a highly educated woman and had Shakespeare at her tongue's end.

"The pulpit of the Presbyterian Church was draped in black, and remained so until Reverend Francis

Herron took charge on April 3, 1811. Old Mr. Graham of Wilkensburg preached the funeral sermon—and afterwards came around to Father and said, 'I say, have you a devil about you?'

" 'Well, I don't know,' replied Father, 'there are plenty about here: are you wanting one?'

"It proved to be some particular kind of a plow Mr. Graham wished to borrow.

"A while back I mentioned 'Harris, the bell ringer.' If this man ever had any other name it has been forgotten; he was always called that. He was sexton of the Presbyterian Church and rang the bell for church and day school. The bell was not at the church, but at the Court House, and did service for all the town. It was not put up until some years after the Court House was built.

"There was a burying ground adjoining the church, and Mr. Steele was interred there. Permits for burying in this graveyard were issued by the church authorities, and the money so collected went to Squire Wilkins. Some of the church members were dubious as to where the money went after that, but they assured themselves that it didn't go to mending the fence surrounding the church, which was then in a state of disrepair. This was a sore subject of conversation among the older ladies, one of whom went so far as to remark to Mother that these permits were a lot like buying a ticket on a ferry boat: 'You get across to the other side but there's no explanation as to what becomes of the cash!' "

These little side glances are indicative of a growth which was actively in progress up and down the valley of the Allegheny during the girlhood of Mary Anderson Way. Similar tales, enacted by other characters, might be related of early Freeport, Kittanning, Franklin, Tionesta, Tidioute, Warren, and Olean.

CHAPTER TWELVE

GREAT-GRANDMOTHER MARY ANDERSON WAY had other tales to relate which concern early days in Pittsburgh:

"During the War of 1812, the news from the Great Lakes was brought to Pittsburgh almost daily by courier; relays of horses being provided between Buffalo and Pittsburgh every ten miles. The arrival of the courier by ferry from across the Allegheny River at the foot of Hancock Street created general excitement, as he rode into town blowing his horn.

"On one occasion when news was expected, my brother Paul had large handbills struck off at Snowden's Printing Office, headed 'Terrible Discombuberation!' The wording of the bill was unintelligible jargon. These bills created great excitement, for nobody could read them, and it was stated they were printed in some Indian language.

"On the surrender of Hull, a Captain Snelling who had been in Pittsburgh, refused to give up his sword, and broke it and shed tears of vexation.

"Four British officers captured during the war were kept in the jail on Jail Alley, in Pittsburgh. The jail was kept by a Mrs. (oh, pshaw! her name doesn't come to me now) and her daughters. The latter, at the request of some young Englishmen, invited several Pittsburgh girls to the jail to an entertainment, that the officers might be better able to spend their time

of imprisonment. Polly Knox, a friend of mine, and I were among those invited, but the strong political feelings of our parents prevented our even thinking of going.

"Party politics after the war (and before) were carried to the extreme. My Father wouldn't allow we children to play with 'Tory' children; nay, even speak to them.

"There was a garrison located on the ground between Liberty Street and the Allegheny River, from

Hand Street to Garrison Alley. It was 'out of town.' A high picket fence surrounded the ground, with a great gate opening on Penn Street looking toward the Point: and another across the lot looking up the river. The lower gate had a sentinal house over it and a great flagstaff alongside, upon which every morning a flag was hoisted. In the yard were several blockhouses, six or eight sided, built of heavy hewn logs, with port holes for cannon. Every Fourth of July a large cannon was stationed at the lower gate and fired down Penn Street; the commandant having, the night before, courteously sent word to his nearest neighbor, my Father, to have his house windows open early in the morning lest the concussion break the glass. One of the commandants in the early days was a Colonel Swearingen, and he was very severe with his men, cow-hiding them, and so forth. A committee of citizens protested against it and he either stopped his course or was removed.

"Sailing vessels were built at Pittsburgh when I was a wee girl—large ones, intended for ocean service. One of these, the Senator Ross, was launched from the banks of the Allegheny River at the corner of the lot just below Hand Street. I ran after some of the servants who went to see the sight but became alarmed at the crowd and ran back, which was just as well, for otherwise I would have been punished. Cannons were fired both from the new ship and from Fort Fayette in celebration of the occasion; this was a war vessel built for the Government. It was launched on a Sunday evening. Then it was taken around the Point to the Monongahela

River opposite Colonel O'Hara's residence which was near to Short Street, on Water Street. Soon after that there came a sudden rise in the Monongahela River and a breaking up of the ice, and the new boat was brought back into the Allegheny. I well remember the sailors

had ropes attached to the vessel, and ran with them along the bank striving to keep the vessel in toward shore, as she was forced up the Allegheny by a reverse current induced by the sudden rise in the Monongahela. This rise must have been very sudden and forcible, as the ice was piled up on the Allegheny's banks quite high and in great quantities.

"The first steamboat? Yes, of course I remember it, and also I remember Mr. and Mrs. Nicholas Roosevelt who built it, and their young child. These folks had two riding horses. Mrs. Roosevelt rode out, taking her child in her lap, and accompanied by a servant on foot, leading the horse. I was attending Miss Spencer's school when one day my brother Paul and another young man called to take me to visit the new steamboat before it started down the river. That was in 1811.

"Did you know that a great many of the cannon balls used by Commodore Perry upon Lake Erie in the War of 1812 were made in Pittsburgh? Great wagon-loads of them were hauled overland to the lake. I know of one cannon ball that never got there; it dropped off a wagon at Sewickley Bottoms and was picked up by a very handsome, curly-headed, blue-eyed young man. Who was he? You couldn't guess? Well, you should know: he was the man I later married, Abishai Way."

CHAPTER THIRTEEN

THE Allegheny River, for the bulk of its length, has never been classed as "an excellent waterway of commerce." This is not surprising when you examine the very nature of the stream—for it is a river which is likely to be frozen solid from December until March, with ice piled in great packs and jams at perhaps thirty localities—piled mountain high with great ice blocks thrown into the most jagged contortions by reason of the grinding pressure brought to bear; then comes the annual "spring thaw" in which the

Allegheny rids itself of this frozen constipation in one vast bowel movement which is a frightening spectacle to behold—urged by an enema of melting snow and drizzling rains which rile all the creeks to flood tide and cause a never-ending roar from each gully and ravine. The river stirs uneasily at first, winces, then with no warning whatever delivers itself of ice, drift, flotsam and jetsam, trees, logs, houses, barns, haystacks, cornshocks, barrels, dead pigs, bloated horses, boxes, barrels, packing crates, and other impedimenta which it has warehoused during the winter—all of this hodge-podge starts moving to the tune of thunderous cannonading of ice jams breaking, and one jam swoops down upon another, and with a continued crashing and rending the mighty discharge is on its way, now taking out bridges, piers, sometimes whole villages, with the natives of the bottom lands fleeing for the hills and terrified livestock jumping fences and racing away for Egypt or anywhere, so as to be shed of this cataclysm. "The Allegheny's bust loose!" This cry is passed from mouth to mouth, and hurries over telegraph wires, and shortly every owner of floating property the entire length of the Ohio River, some 1,000 miles long, is suddenly busy getting his houseboat, or raft, or steamboat, or fleet of barges out of the road of this demon of destruction. For oftentimes the full force of this upheaval runs at brim tide for several days, and the broad Ohio proves a meager plumbing system to handle this cosmic diarrhetic discharge. Not until the Mississippi is reached does the destruction cease, and sometimes not even then—for case-hardened blocks of Allegheny ice have serenely sailed by New Orleans at intervals.

Now comes the "spring flood" brought about by abnormal rainfall over the watershed, and it is March or April. In the course of forty-eight hours the Allegheny has boomed up from a nominal stage of perhaps three feet to 22 feet, or 30 feet—on March 18, 1936, at Pittsburgh, to 46 feet. In hundreds of homes along the "bottom lands" all fires are extinguished, pianos are jacked up on stilts and living-room carpets have three feet of water on them, and outhouses, plankage, garages, more houses, and stuff are sailing along at a speed of from five to twenty miles an hour, bound for the Gulf of Mexico. Not infrequently a barn goes bobbing along with two or three hens roosting on the eaves, or a hound is seen dismally baying from a pile of assorted splinters, and occasionally there is great excitement as a woman or a man is rescued from a house as it sails by.

After this fanfare, the Allegheny River settles down to a "fair boating stage," which means, usually, a slowly falling river, mildly bolstered every week or so by early summer rainfall, and kept at such a stage that the gravel bars and shallow places have from three to ten feet of water over them. This may last until June, but more frequently it doesn't, and wears out by the middle of May.

All summer long, with a few notable historic exceptions, the Allegheny River is a big, overgrown creek, spilling out its contribution of crystal-clear water to the Ohio River. The long, slender, rolling gravel bars come out for air, and the catfish have to stand on their heads to keep their gills wet. The Allegheny River in summer is one of the beauty spots of Creation, but totally useless for navigation purposes.

At some unpredictable date in the fall, ranging anywhere from the middle of September until Thanksgiving, the fall rains set in and bolster the Allegheny back to a navigable stage which, if luck is good, may last until the first "northwester" sings through the tall pines and freezes everything up again tight as a clam.

This vicious circle of events goes on year after year with such deadly certainty that anybody wishing to invest money in an Allegheny River navigation enterprise must be quite certain that three months' activity out of a possible twelve will bring him out of the red and leave a profit balance—then perhaps, and just perhaps, the old River will allow him an extra month every year or so "for gravy." Take a proposition of this sort to your banker and see what he thinks of it; and if your banker lends you ten thousand dollars to build you a steamboat to operate from Oil City to Pittsburgh, please wire the author his address, for there are several schemes pigeonholed in my desk which may interest him—I don't want his advice, I want his money. Liberal commission will be allowed.

Even our great-grandfathers viewed the Allegheny River with their heads cocked over and one eye shut when it came to making financial investments.

Best proof of this lies in the construction of the Pennsylvania Canal, a state project built to link Philadelphia and Pittsburgh before the days of railroads and to afford "lightning" service in the transportation of passengers and freight. The route of this canal brought it to the banks of the Allegheny River from the east at the mouth of the Kiskiminetas River, some 30 miles above Pittsburgh. Now, it is axiomatic that the best portion of any river from a navigation standpoint is on its lower reaches; yet even on that comparatively tame 30-mile stretch from Freeport to Pittsburgh, with a depth sufficient for canalboats, the Pennsylvania Canal authorities voted an emphatic thumbs down on utilizing it. Instead, they spent a fabulous fortune of taxpayers' money piping the canal across the Allegheny River on an aqueduct below the mouth of the Kiski River, and hired umteen-hundred Irishman to dig the canal down along the north bank of the Allegheny River to Pittsburgh, where another aqueduct was constructed to pipe it over into the city. Two or three dams of masonry with convenient locks built in the Allegheny River proper would have done the job to a nicety but oh, no! Not by a jugful! Only nitwits would trust a transportation enterprise to the caprices and annual bowel movements of La Belle Rivière.

Yet, with all these drawbacks, if we were to print here a roster of the men who have made a profession of navigating the Allegheny River, engaged in commerical enterprises, there would be no room left for another chapter—for such a listing would amply fill this book!

CHAPTER FOURTEEN

INHABITANTS along the shores of a lazy river with a sluggish current in it become affected by the very temper of the stream; such persons are apt to be as indolent as their river, and it follows that most of the slow-moving people of the United States live in the southern coastal regions where the rivers are sticky, muddy, lethargic; slinking along with sleepy monotony; never arousing themselves, under any circumstance, to quick and decisive action. The Mississippi is sometimes said to "be on a rampage" as it dissolves levees from the delta country on out to the jetties, but this is a mistaken notion, largely: the Mississippi never rampages. It rises with a slow stealth, day by day, week by week, and mud water creeps back into bayous and creeks—inching back, inching, inching—offering a warning weeks ahead of what may come; it "stands" at flood tide for days at a time, sopping and wetting everything in reach and covering the landscape with a layer of the best chocolate fudge—it does this with such a sound-asleep monotony that even the jack rabbits can't stand it, and go daffy from sheer boredom. Powerful steamboats push laden barges upstream on the Mississippi so slowly that a leadsman out on the head of a long tow of barges one time hollered back to the pilot and said, "A hen just laid an egg in the bushes out abreast of here, and an old cluck came along and is settin' on it." This pilot changed watches with his partner so many times that he had forgotten the incident when one day the fireman called up the steps to the pilothouse and said, "Say, there's a brood of chicks out here in the bushes that's just been hatched." Another interval of time went by and one afternoon the engineer called up through the speaking tube and said, "Say, Mr. Pilot, stop the boat a minute —I was just out oiling on the fantail and noticed some springers out on the shore—think I can pop a couple of 'em off with my thirty-two." Slow motion there in the south country, and any semblance of a "rampage" or "booming river" comes from artificial interference with sluggish streams—mostly from the levee system.

The unpredictable, stand-on-its-head tactics of the Allegheny River, with its sudden ups and downs and seasons of racing currents and ice floes and attendant destruction, caused the valley to become populated with a singularly virile race of people. The Allegheny River, in early times, could not be utilized for navigation purposes in summer and fall when the weather was good; no, it was in the roughest months of the year that commerce teemed; it was in March, with the wind blowing great guns; it was in April, when one day might produce snow, wind, rain, sunshine and a dull chill; it was in November and December, in times of snow and northwesters that the Allegheny boatman was in business. He necessarily acquired a cast-iron constitution. Here are a few accounts of him:

Said a passenger on an Allegheny River packet in 1850:

"These lumbermen are about the finest specimens of robust, healthy men we have ever beheld. Like the tall trees of their native forests, they grow up firm and erect, full of vigor, strength, and manhood. Theirs is truly a hard life, but they have enjoyments, as well as other people. When away from home, the lumbermen take a little license sometimes, and play and frolic like children let loose from school, but there is no malice in their composition and at home they are as orderly a set of men as can be found anywhere."

A traveler fresh arrived in Warren, Pennsylvania, in the eighteen-forties found the streets teeming with raftsmen, and wrote perhaps the best descriptive information on record:

"Main Street, which runs along the verge of the precipitous bank . . . was swarming with raftsmen in every variety of costume. Some had the old drab, or rather dirty yellow, greatcoat of their grandfather's times, surmounted with its pyramids of capes, and narrow, turned-over, threadbare velvet collar, thrown loosely over their shoulders, and fastened at the throat with a clasp, while the shriveled arms, cuffless and torn, swung back and forth or were borne about in the wind. Those wearing this antiquated garment were generally tall, gaunt fellows, with a napless and unrimmed hat, whose crown, hanging to one side like a valve, fell in and afforded a ventilation, or swung gracefully on the outside, like the guerdon of ancient knights; while their long, cane-like legs were enveloped in trousers patched and bagging, and their pedals in boots which would scarcely shrink beside Frances' lifeboats. Others wore sealcaps with the front piece torn off, or turned up, a loose coat with the skirt torn off, or with both thrown over their shoulders. Here and there, thinly scattered through the crowd, might be seen, soiled and faded, the fashions of last year hurrying along, or surrounded with a group of tatterdemalions, pretty surely indicating the lumber owner; while about one in four had a joint of bacon under one arm, or handkerchiefs full of bread in each hand, while the sun flashed brightly on the scores of tin pails, coffee pots and cups scattered profusely through the crowd."

This picturesque collection of hardy men floated lumber out of the Allegheny River during the heyday of that traffic, which covered the period from the 1840's through the Civil War. They brought rafts of logs oftentimes, to be sawed at mills on the lower rivers. Frequently these log rafts were piled high with sawed lumber, shingles, and hardwoods in various stages of finish. Hardwoods, such as oak and hickory, would not float and had to be carried as cargo.

"Dropping" a lumber raft out from Olean to Pittsburgh sounds prosaic and stupidly dull, I know, and the trouble lies, I think, in the fact that there existed no "literary" raftsmen to write down the excitement and the zest of the profession. Those few raftsmen who have scribbled their recollections seem to be most concerned with bragging of the immensity of individual rafts which they "rode out," and in order to magnify individual prowess and skill, these accounts are necessarily devoid of harrowing escapes or misadventures. A truly great raftsman, who knew his business, didn't have misadventures: he made his living by guiding his rafts through thick and thin in complete safety; that is, as far as the outside world need know about his affairs. If you would hear stirring stories of ocean travel, do not hunt up the captain of an ocean liner—his tongue will congeal into concrete when you mention such matters to him, if he is a true-blue skipper, that is: and do not seek to see the notes in his log-book even—for they will prove to be statistical notes concerning speed, weather, and ports of call, and tell you nothing of what you want to know. Fact is, a usual "Log Book" is about as hair-raising as the telephone directory, and most seasoned navigators are as devoid of harrowing stories of courage and fortitude as your family dentist. Only when safe among their own kind do mariners of any stripe let down the gates and admit their shortcomings and admit the perplexities they have drifted into through mistakes in their own judgment.

I never saw a log raft on the Allegheny River: I was born too late for that. However, in my younger days there were plenty of them down on Big Sandy River, and strewn along the Ohio River from Catlettsburg to Cincinnati. This timber came from the Tug and Levisa forks of the Big Sandy, from away up in the Kentucky mountains, and it was floated to the Crane sawmill located across from Cincinnati's East End, where a huge derrick lifted the "sticks" from the river and transferred them to railroad cars, I think. Most times these rafts were towed down to the mill in charge of a steam towboat—one of these towboats was the *Crown Hill*.

Once the Ohio River had a "pop" raise in the middle of summer about this time, anyhow I was "mud" clerk on a combination freight and passenger boat plying between Cincinnati and Pittsburgh. We had just finished loading at Cincinnati and were about ready to depart for the 468-mile journey to the headwaters of the Ohio when an official of the Crane Lumber Company called by telephone and warned us that a log raft had broken loose from its moorings in East End and was drifting down our direction and there was a chance of its poking into our affairs there at the wharf and causing some damage.

Our captain hurried to the pilothouse with this intelligence and relayed the news to Dayton Randolph, our pilot. Dayton advised the captain to back the boat away from the landing immediately, and to let him get out in the stream, and above the two bridges which were just above our landing place, before the runaway raft arrived. "If that raft hits a bridge pier it may round-to, and hard to tell what way it will go," added Dayton.

The captain rang the roof bell and ordered the mate to let go the lines, and in another moment we were out in the middle of the Ohio River. I stayed up in the pilothouse to see the show. Apparently no raft was in sight. Dayton was a cautious soul, and went up the Kentucky shore, and under the Central Bridge. Soon as the river unfolded ahead of us now, sure enough a long, black-looking form was seen lurking along the Ohio shore above the L. & N. Railroad bridge. It was the runaway log raft. It was more than that; it had men on it, and two other fellows were in a skiff rowing for all their might and getting nowhere. "They've got a rope hitched from that skiff to the head of the raft," commented Dayton, "trying to pull it out in the river to miss the shore pier of the L. & N. bridge." Yes, that was it, without a shadow of doubt.

This big island of lumber seemed to be going insufferably slowly through the water, not nearly so fast as the current, it seemed, and the men on the raft, three of them, were doing nothing to speak about—apparently unwilling passengers on an excursion they had not anticipated.

Dayton said there was nothing our boat could do either to be a help or a hindrance, so he pulled the stopping bell and turned our steamer into a grandstand from which to watch proceedings.

The closer down to the L. & N. bridge the raft came, the more obvious it appeared she was going to hit the shore pier, fashioned from solid stone—head on. The men plying the oars in the skiff sensed the peril also, sooner than we did, I suspect, and redoubled their efforts to pull the head of the acreage of timber out into the river to miss this obstruction. Their enthusiasm was creditable, but the plight of the marooned men on the raft was more dramatic—they foresaw what was about to happen and could do nothing about the matter, so there they stood, a little forward of the center of the raft, a group of cigar-store Indians.

Twenty feet, fifteen feet, ten feet—then a week went by in the next few instants—and we saw a pile of jackstraws fly in all directions at the head of the raft as it connected with the bridge pier. Sixty-foot timbers jumped like mammoth frogs into the air, and scattered all around, and frothed the river into a lather with their wrenchings and splashings. The men on the raft commenced running aft on it, away from the destruction, and the fellows in the skiff disappeared for a moment in the commotion, then emerged again, still rowing, now free of the raft, for the rope which held them had parted.

The three raft-bound fellows were plenty anxious to leave there now, and they were jumping up and down, and waving their arms, and yelling "Hey!" and "Help!" and such things, hoping to attract the attention of the momentarily bewildered men in the skiff. The bridge pier was a huge plow coming straight up through the center of the raft, shedding logs to either side, tearing and jerking the whole affair to shreds and bits.

With about time enough left for two whoops and

a holler, the occupants of the skiff realized the plight of their friends, and executed a neat maneuver with dexterous handling of their boat, brought the stern of it around to the raft, or what was left of it by this time, close enough for three grateful human beings to jump aboard and get away. A few more rumbles and a roar, and the raft was reduced to drift and kindling. Dayton pulled the "come-ahead" bell and we went on up the river.

Entered in our steamer's logbook that night was this item: "Left Cincinnati fifteen minutes early a/c log raft broke loose." Wouldn't that make fine reading for some historian someday?

On the Allegheny River, such happenings as we have just reported were frequent. Here is an item clipped from an issue of the Pittsburgh *Gazette* in early May, 1852:

"The Allegheny is covered with floating fragments of rafts, valuable timber of all descriptions, which have been swept away from their moorings and now mingle in the wild confusion with trees, driftwood and fence rails. Numbers of human beings have been seen on rafts, as they have been swept past the city, clinging to their property at the peril of their lives. Altogether there must have been sixty-five rafts floating at the same time, within a distance of a few miles. We stood upon the St. Clair [later Sixth Street] bridge as the rafts were coming down and the scene was as unparalleled as it was deplorable. The entire surface of the river was thickly dotted with unbroken rafts, fragments of rafts and isolated logs and boards. Some of the rafts had three or four men on board, some two, some one, and many were guided only by the current of the stream. The latter were almost sure to strike a bridge pier, and the collisions invariably separated them into still smaller fragments. We saw probably a dozen that were manned strike upon the piers, and in several instances the courageous raftsmen were compelled to leap from one fragment to another to avoid being hurled amidst the crashing timbers. The coolness and self-possession of the hardy raftsmen was marked and admired by the hundreds who witnessed the unusual scene from the bridges and shores."

What do you suppose those cool and self-possessed raftsmen did that night in town? Drink ice-cream sodas? Hardly—for it strikes me ice-cream sodas had not been invented those days. With all my soul I envy them.

CHAPTER FIFTEEN

EARLY-DAY raftsmen and lumbermen saw some of the pioneer wildlife of the Allegheny regions, but not the full tide of it, by any means. The American bison (the animal on the "buffalo nickel") formerly frequented the upper watersheds, but he was a novelty back as far as "early settler" times. Even in 1806 the buffalo was a legend on the upper Allegheny. An old man, one of the first settlers on Conewango, built his log house on the immediate borders of a salt spring (perhaps on Onondargo Lake, near Chautauqua—nobody knows for sure). The first several seasons there, he was paid regular visits by the buffaloes; they traveled in single file always following each other at regular distances, forming droves on their arrival, of about three hundred each. The first and second years, so unacquainted were these poor brutes with this man's house or with his nature, that within a few hours they rubbed the house completely down, taking delight in turning the logs of wood off with their horns, while he had some difficulty to escape from being trampled under their feet or crushed to death in his own ruins. At

that period he supposed there could not have been less than ten thousand in the neighborhood of the spring. They sought for no manner of food but only bathed and drank three or four times a day and rolled in the earth, or reposed, with their flanks distended, in the adjacent shades, and on the fifth and sixth days separated into distinct droves, bathed, drank, and departed in single file, according to the exact order of their arrival. They all rolled successively in the same hole and each thus carried away a coat of mud to preserve the moisture of their skin, and which when hardened and baked by the sun, would resist the stings of millions of insects that otherwise would persecute these peaceful travelers to madness or even death.

In the first and second years this old man with some companions killed from six to seven hundred of these noble creatures, merely for the sake of the skins, which to them were worth only two shillings each, and after this "work of death" they were obliged to leave the place till the following season, or till the wolves, bears, panthers, eagles, rooks, ravens, had devoured the carcasses, and abandoned the place for other prey. In the two following years, the same persons killed great numbers out of the first two droves that arrived, skinned them, and left the bodies exposed to the sun and air; but they soon had reason to repent of this; for the remaining droves, as they came up in succession, stopped, gazed on the mangled and putrid bodies, sorrowfully moaned or furiously lowed aloud, and returned instantly to the wilderness in an unusual run, without tasting their favorite spring or licking the impregnated earth; nor did they, or any of their race, ever revisit the neighborhood.

Among the scraps of buffalo lore is the fact that the French called French Creek "La Bouffe Rivière" because of the buffaloes found there. Throughout the Allegheny valley today are various streams named Buffalo Creek for the same reason.

Bull elks weighing 1,000 to 1,200 pounds roamed the Allegheny forests until Civil War times. In the hills which border the Allegheny River are frequent outcroppings of rock—sometimes away up on lofty heights—and these were known as "elk rocks" in earlier days. It was the habit of the hunted elk, when pursued, to make a last stand on one of these rocks. Mounting it, and facing the foe, Sir Elk went to work with jabs from his forefeet and kicks from his hind legs, to reduce the enemy. Hunters frequently found dead wolves lying about the bases of these jagged rock outcroppings, mute evidence of battle. Sometimes Sir Elk was not the victor; once in a while his stripped skeleton lay among the whitening wolf bones.

Up at Gardeau, some years ago, there was a veteran hunter named Colonel Parker; without a shadow of doubt the colonel knew as much about Pennsylvania elk as any man who ever followed a trail, although some of his neighbors passed knowing looks to one another regarding his relation of personal exploits. Just the same, the colonel swore up and down that his story of the biggest set of antlers ever captured in a Pennsylvania woods was straight as a ramrod.

"That set of antlers was secured in the Kettle Creek country," related the colonel. "Major Isaac Lyman, Philip Tome, George Ayers, L. D. Spoffard, and William Wattles were in the party. Philip Tome was a great hunter, and the famous interpreter for Cornplanter and Blacksnake, the great Indian chiefs. He came over from Warren County to help Major Lyman capture an elk alive, and the party started out on the first snow, with plenty of ropes and things. They camped, but the elk were in such big herds that they couldn't get a chance at a single bull for more than a week. Then they got the biggest one they ever saw and gave chase to him. They started him from his bed on Yocum Hill. The dogs took him down Little Kettle Creek to Big Kettle, and up that two or three miles. There the elk came to bay on one of those 'elk rocks.' Tome kept the dogs at a distance until the hunters came up, and meanwhile Mr. Elk left the rock and lit out for other places. Tome said, 'No need to go further; he'll come back here to this rock.' Tome knew about elk habits. So the party dropped some slender trees, made poles, and fitted up some nooses of rope. After about five or six hours waiting around, there came a crashing through the woods, down the side of the mountain, and a yelping of the dogs, and sure enough here came Mr. Elk back to his rock. He got out on it, faced around, and commenced clawing dogs—funny, he didn't seem to mind the hunters at all. The fellows got the noose over his big antlers, pulled up the slack, and made the ends fast to some big trees. By some good work these hunters got that elk to the Allegheny River, and floated him on a raft down to Olean. Oh, they had a prize, all right! They took him up through New York State to Albany, and showed him off for pay, and made a barrel of money, and sold him for five hundred dollars. That elk stood sixteen hands high and had antlers six feet long, and eleven points on each side."

One of the last survivors (perhaps the very last elk) was tracked by an Indian through a blinding snowstorm to the wilds of Clarion County, where the elk came to bay on an elk rock there, the last-stand defense he knew about. He turned, surveyed his enemy as of yore, there was a sharp rifle crack, and the days of elk in Pennsylvania were over. This was in the winter of 1867. Jim Jacobs was the Indian—from the Cattaraugus reservation. No elk had been seen for several years prior to this occurrence.

The panther had disappeared from the Allegheny regions before this final elk met his doom, and lynx were just about at the point of extinction. Tom Fenton was hunting deer on Kinzua Creek about the same time Jim Jacobs shot the last elk in Clarion County. Fenton shot a deer and hung the forequarters up on a tree. Next day he returned for the meat but found some animal had made a meal of it. The tracks in the snow indicated the animal had sprung from a distance fully ten feet from the base of the tree, and this was most interesting, so Fenton set a trap. Returning later, the trap and clog were gone, but fresh tracks were clearly indicated, and Fenton found the animal up a tree, trap and all. The chain was wound around a large limb twice, and there—30 feet above the ground—was a Canadian lynx, weighing about 40 pounds, dead, frozen stiff. The animal was considerably taller than a wildcat, longer of body, of a light gray, tail 6 to 8 inches in length, and the funniest thing about it was the ears, which had stiff black hairs coming out from the inside and coming to a point at the end of the ears, then twisting around like an old-fashioned horsehair fish line for about three-quarters of an inch. Right atop of this was formed a round ball of the black hair about as big as a blue plum, so that when the head was held up and shaken, the little bells on top of the ears jumped around in all shapes.

The timber wolf went quickly, especially after various counties of the state offered a bounty for each one brought in. McKean County paid $25 for a grown wolf and $12 for each whelp. The payment of these bounties gave rise to many a cry of "wolf!" which, upon investigation, turned out to be a dog or some other hoax perpetrated by a needy hunter—needy of twenty-five dollars. Nevertheless, nobody is too sure about the wolf's total extinction in the wilds of the Allegheny even today; just about the time they all seem dead and gone, somebody has an experience with what he believes to be a genuine wolf.

With such rapid and alarming disappearance of wildlife, it is no small wonder that the common little skunk remains at his usual stand. In daytime the creature is so shortsighted that he will almost run into a person before discovering the mistake; he is absent-minded, blundering, and curious. The skunk has long been a robber of hens' nests and a fancier of poultry. Moreover, he is susceptible to hydrophobia. Yet he survives; more than that—he abounds. How he has managed is his own secret, apparently. This survival is also true of the black bear which, in forested hills, seems as plentiful as ever.

Deer, protected by law, have increased in the Allegheny valley until they are a nuisance in places.

In varying numbers, and in localities favorable to their habits, are found gray squirrels, and black, and red; chipmunks galore; ground hogs; some beaver—although not plentiful; muskrats; a few porcupines; rabbits of various breeds and varieties; wild cats, fox, otters, mink, weasel, sable, and raccoon. In the streams the old mossback catfish still is plentiful, and bass, and trout—although these latter two have been given "state aid" and nourished along.

Copperhead snakes frequent the entire Allegheny valley and are sufficiently abundant, even today, to require great care on the part of persons who would walk through tall weeds and grassy places.

Something about the hillsides, the rocks, and the general climate of the Allegheny regions between Oil City and Warren has been especially attractive to the multiplication of rattlesnakes. This area early became noted as one of the most prolific snake territories on the globe. Timber rattlers grew to healthy proportions and, when disturbed, would set up a buzzing equaled only by a plague of locusts. Many of them were weeded out by a single human being who became noted as "Rattlesnake Pete." Pete Gruber, who won this acclaim, ran a combination museum and saloon in Oil City about the turn of the century. In the museum was a model of an oil producer's farm in full blast, with everything working, and W. N. Y. & P. tank cars and engines moving around, oil-well jacks pumping, and so on. Pete was somewhat of a practical joker and went to extreme pains to rig his exhibits; one time he had a door marked ENTRANCE which, when opened, disclosed a real human skeleton. But Pete's main enterprise had to do with snake catching.

He had been bitten by rattlesnakes no less than eighteen times and, as a result, had passed a good deal of his time in hospitals, swathed in bandages, and enduring the most agonizing pains. Gradually he evolved a method for his labor of love, which he described this way: "Whenever I am bitten now, I never suck a wound. If there is any slight superficial wound in a person's mouth, such as a scratch, the venom would thus get into the system and prove fatal. Directly I have been bitten I cut around the puncture and make another wound between the injured spot and the heart with a sharp knife, which I always carry with me in case of such an emergency. Into these two self-inflicted wounds I then inject permanganate of potash, which has the effect of nullifying the serpent's venom."

Pete went over so well in Oil City that he soon

got too rich for that town and moved to Rochester, New York, where he owned a big automobile in 1911 equipped with a rattlesnake headlight on each fender, holding red and green signal lights. Peter was well known and liked by the police officers and drove around town at night with no lights showing other than these glowing snakes.

CHAPTER SIXTEEN

THE next commotion in the Allegheny valley was caused by a scarcity of whales. Unfortunately for that mammal, the human race had long since discovered he was a floating oil refinery. By 1850, better than six hundred vessels manned by Captain Ahabs were prowling the seas, harpoons raised, taking the slack out of the Moby Dick population with triumphant success. Whale oil became expensive—so very expensive that healthy dividends were being realized by distilling "coal oil" from coal. A number of plants engaged in this industry sprang up in eastern United States. Some of the more enterprising distillers had discovered a short cut in utilizing a slimy ooze variously called "Seneca Oil" or petroleum which abounded in "spots" along the Allegheny River, and in Kentucky, and Virginia, and other places. In 1850, also, an imaginary pencil dot called "the center of population" had assumed the speed of a comet and was racing over hill and dale along the line of the 39th parallel; since the day George Washington fell into the Allegheny River this dot had moved from the eastern seaboard to the hogweeds on the Little Kanawha River back of Parkersburg: the westward motion of this pencil dot was requiring a great deal of axle grease and night illumination, and the task of supplying the demand was rapidly falling short of the ability to deliver. The slaughter of whales was furious and relentless, but not enough. Then a rail-

road conductor from the New York & New Haven put down his ticket punch, came to the valley of the Allegheny, and gave the world its third largest industry. He found all the oil anybody could possibly want. This fellow's name was Drake. His story is an interesting one.

Edwin L. Drake was raised on a Vermont farm but didn't like the work, or perhaps was too frail to endure the rigors of such a life, and at the age of eighteen started a shifting career in which he once clerked a night boat between Buffalo and Detroit, again he spent two years in a Michigan hotel, and later he clerked in a dry goods store in New Haven, clerked in New York—and got married there—and became an express agent on the Boston & Albany railroad. In 1849 he was promoted to conductor on the New York & New Haven. While punching tickets here his wife died, leaving one child; he gave up his home, went to "batch" in a New Haven hotel. Here he met James M. Townsend, who persuaded Drake to draw his savings of $200 from the bank, invest it in Pennsylvania Rock Oil Company stock. No fortune ensued, and Drake continued punching with care the ticket of the passengaire, and married again in 1857, got sick, had to quit his job. This tragedy suddenly took an ironic tangent . . . as seems often the case with persons other than ourselves.

James M. Townsend, the oil-promoter, instead of running true to storybook pattern, and becoming the villain who fleeced our honest and unsuspecting hero out of his hard-earned life savings, now turned himself into a magnificent benefactor: he heard of Edwin L. Drake's plight, and sent him on a journey for pay—to serve the double purpose of recuperating his health and investigating the oil deposits in the Allegheny valley! Drake accepted at once, stopped off in Syracuse to see the salt wells there, and rattled into Titusville, Pennsylvania, aboard the stagecoach from Erie one day in mid-December, 1857. After several days spent in snooping around this locality, he went down to Tarentum and saw the salt wells there, and returned immediately to Connecticut with a plan for operating an oil spring near Titusville which the Pennsylvania Rock Oil Company, of which Mr. Townsend was president, owned.

Early the following spring the Seneca Oil Company was formed, with "Colonel" Drake (by which title Mr. Townsend had addressed mail to him during the first stay in Titusville) as president and owner of one-fortieth of the stock—rather one-fortieth of the ownership, inasmuch as stock was not issued, for the company was in reality a partnership working under the laws governing joint-stock associations.

Provided with a fund of a thousand dollars as a starter, Drake was engaged at a thousand dollars a year to begin operations. Early in May, 1858, he and his family arrived in Titusville and were quartered at the American Hotel, which boarded the colonel, Mrs. Drake, two children and a horse for $6.50 per week. The oil to be "worked" was seeping from a well, or hole, on a small island in Oil Creek, near Titusville—this being the same property originally acquired by the Pennsylvania Rock Oil Company, and now held by the newly formed Seneca Oil Company. As an inkling of how Colonel Drake originally planned to "work" this holding, suffice to say that he went to considerable trouble procuring some picks and shovels.

Pick-and-shovel methods resulted in a shallow well on the island which produced ten gallons of oil daily by the end of June. But Colonel Drake hadn't been looking at salt wells for entertainment; he had a deep-seated notion that such a well drilled near this oozing spring would greatly facilitate the flow. The next job was to find a steam engine to furnish the necessary

power for the drilling operations. After going up several blind alleys with the attendant loss of time and money, Drake finally located a fellow named William A. Smith in Franklin, Pennsylvania, who made tools for cleaning salt wells, and a contract was arranged to furnish an outfit—which did not require a steam plant for its operation. On May 20th the tools were delivered at the small island on Oil Creek, meanwhile Drake having completed a pump house and derrick.

Even then delays and tribulations had not retreated from the field. John J. McLaurin, from whose written recollections of early days in the oil country we have already heavily borrowed, tells the exciting story this way:

"In artesian-boring it is necessary to drill in rock. Mrs. Glasse's old-time cook-book gained celebrity by starting a recipe for rabbit pie: 'First catch your hare.' The principle applies to artesian drilling: 'First catch your rock.' The ordinary rule was to dig a pit or well-hole to the rock and crib it with timber. 'Uncle Billy' Smith and his sons [the same Franklin man who built the tools] contracted to drill the well for Drake; first they dug a few feet, but the hole filled with water and continually caved in. A council-of-war was held, at which Drake recommended driving an iron tube through the clay and quicksand to the rock. This was effectual. Colonel Drake should have patented the process, which was his exclusive device and decidedly valuable. The pipe was driven sixty-three feet to hard pan and the drill started on August 14th. The workmen averaged three feet a day, resting at night and on Sundays. Indications of oil were met as the tools pierced the rock. Drake's backers did not deluge him with money, being tired from repeated postponements, and Drake himself was not 'well heeled' due to losing speculations and sickness. Yet he had the courage of his convictions, and managed to borrow $600 from a Titusville merchant to tide over the crisis. The tools pursued the downward road. . . .

"On Saturday afternoon, August 28, 1859, the well had reached the depth of 69 feet, in a coarse sand. Smith and his sons concluded to 'lay off' until Monday morning. As they were about to quit the drill dropped six inches into a crevice such as was common in salt wells. Nothing was thought of this circumstance, the tools were drawn out and all hands adjourned to Titusville. Mr. Smith went to the well on Sunday afternoon to see if it had moved away or been purloined during the night. Peering into the hole he saw fluid within eight or ten feet. A piece of tin spouting was lying outside. He plugged one end of this spouting, let it down by a string, and pulled it up. His improvised bucket was full of—muddy water? No! It was filled with PETROLEUM!

"Not daring to leave the well now, Uncle Billy lowered the spouting again and again, each time bringing up a cargo of oil. A straggler out for a Sunday stroll approached, heard the story, sniffed the oil, and bore the tidings to the village. When Colonel Drake came down bright and early Monday morning, the Smith clan were guarding three barrels of the precious liquid. By noon the pumping apparatus was adjusted and the well commenced producing at the rate of twenty barrels a day!

"A ten-gallon-daily proposition turned into over a six-hundred-gallon-daily bonanza! Lights, lamps and lanterns all over the world needed this ooze; axles on dusty roads squeaked for it from Maine to Nebraska; new-fangled railroads needed oil. Here it was—coming out of a piece of three-inch pipe driven into a 70-foot hole in the ground.

"This excitement happened at the head of Oil Creek—a crooked stream of little or no consequence which meanders some twenty miles down from the vicinity of Titusville to the Allegheny River, emptying in at Oil City, Pa. In 1859 there was no Oil City, Pa. —merely a collection of shambily houses and a store or two, and this collection of next-to-nothingness was called 'Cornplanter,' to honor the old Indian chieftain of the neighborhood who drew considerable water while he was alive—taking active part in influencing the 'braves' of the upper Allegheny regions during Revolutionary times. Chief Cornplanter had been dead a good long time in 1859 (twenty years anyhow—maybe more) and the 'town' which bore his name wasn't much better off—half dead; two-thirds perhaps—for there was slim prospect of the place amounting to anything.

"A year later a CITY had grown up where Cornplanter was; a regular booming city with banks, stores, mills, good people and bad—and everybody and everything had two things in common—an enthusiastic interest in the oil business and a layer of greasy mud. Three items dominate the lower Mississippi valley; niggers, mules, and mud. Two things dominated the Oil Creek regions those days; oil and mud.

"Oil and mud; mud and oil. Grease, clay, ooze, mire, muck. Filth, stench, grime, dirt. Up Oil Creek is where the stranger saw a hat in the road, lifted it up with a stick, discovered a man under it. 'Howdy, stranger,' said the man's head which had been uncovered. The stranger stammered, 'Why, you are buried in mud —up to your ears.' With a grimace, the native replied, 'That ain't nothing; I'm riding a horse.' "

This was the beginning of Oil City, Pennsylvania.

CHAPTER SEVENTEEN

An oil well is an exciting-looking affair, and its general getup has not altered materially since it first went into business—a whole lot like a railroad caboose in this respect—hence a description of an 1861 oil well would serve to identify an oil pumper built in 1871 or in 1891—or in 1941, if we make some minor substitutions and replace a good bit of the original wooden structure with steel tubing and framing.

A person unacquainted with an oil well, and coming upon one of them, might first mistake it for a "fire tower" of the Forestry Service. A huge frame structure rises above the treetops, and goes up and up, sometimes 60 or 80 feet, getting narrower in dimension as it rises, until at the top there is hardly room to set a meal for four hungry children. This imposing tower, or "derrick" as it is called in the oil country, may be 20 feet square at the base, and all the way aloft are wooden braces and cross braces, and on one side is a narrow wooden ladder running from the bottom to the tiptop of the structure. No boy or girl in the oil country passes his (or her) fifth birthday without having climbed to the extreme tiptop of an oil derrick.

Most daring young adventurers do this stunt on a windy day, for the thrill of the triumph is then trebled. Going to heaven could, at best, be but a mild experience to any child after his initial experience aloft on a derrick ladder. These ladders, doubtless, aside from their utili-

tarian value, claim the distinction of putting more gray hairs on mothers' heads than any other single item in the oil-field country.

The hole-in-the-ground whence the oil is pumped is located plumb under this derrick affair—and once "ile" has been struck, and the well set to pumping, the big derrick is useless baggage—for the derrick is put up in the first place to handle the casing and long lengths of pipe and tools used in the drilling operations. Yet, the derrick is usually allowed to stand; who can tell, there may come a day when the well will need deepening, or cleaning, or repairing.

The usual well is pumped on the "walking beam" principle, same as an old-time Hudson River steamboat, with a large hewn timber seesawing up and down with slow and painful motions, creaking and protesting continually, and getting its impulse from a "one-lunger" gas engine housed in a shed and connected by belts to an enormous wheel. There sometimes is a device attached to the exhaust from this engine which causes each muffled explosion to utter a croak. This uncanny "creo-ok creo-ok creo-ok creo-ok" sound is audible at least as far as the home of the owner of the oil well, and he can sit in his parlor and read his newspaper, with his ear tuned to this sound. When it stops for any reason, he knows something is the matter with the oil well, and he goes to investigate.

While a well is being drilled there is a steam boiler somewhere in the vicinity—housed in a shed sometimes—and always at a safe distance. Usually the boiler is taken away after the drilling is finished, for there is no further use for it then and it may be of service somewhere else. Typical of all wells is an entire absence of paint—all the woodwork is raw and unadorned—and an air of unkempt appearance, for oil wells are slovenly things, and always the peculiarly pungent aroma of fresh crude—a smell something like a mixture of gasoline and tar. Add to these things a big wooden tank or so to hold the oil (with a convenient ladder for curious children) and you have a general idea of any one of the thousands and thousands of such structures which dot the landscape in the Allegheny River regions. These oil wells may be found in creek bottoms, on the sides of hills, on the highest hilltops, in woods, in oatfields, in graveyards, on front lawns, in city property—almost anywhere—for, like bad weeds, they are not particular where they take root.

There was no science to locating oil wells in the early times along the Allegheny; a story is told of a fellow named Kepler who continually dreamed of an Indian menacing him with bow and arrow. One night while this dream was going on a young lady arrived on the scene (in the dream, of course) and handed Kepler a loaded rifle. Kepler let fly at the redskin, missed him, but made a considerable hole in the ground where the Indian had just been. Lo and behold: oil gushed from this blasted terra firma! Not long after this, Kepler visited an oil property he was interested in, and recognized the spot where he shot at the Indian in his dream.

A well was drilled on the strength of this dream (this is a true story, so they report in the valley of the Allegheny) and a gusher came in to the tune of twelve hundred barrels a day, and soon settled down to delivering an average of eight hundred barrels daily for a year. The first cargo of ten thousand barrels brought $90,000, representing ten days' production. Other wells were drilled on the property and Kepler and his associates skimmed off a neat $8,000,000 (some say nearer $10,000,000) which, so some fellow figured, in silver dollars is enough money to load a freight train or build a column twenty miles high. Some dream.

Little Oil Creek valley has seen several fortunes made and lost. One of the queerest examples, perhaps, is the case of Widow McClintock, a farmer woman whose husband died just as the excitement started. Widow McClintock leased her properties and went on about her daily chores. When the money came in, in good sound cash, she secreted it at various places about the house. Her job in life was to raise her grandson, John W. Steele—then a lad in his teens—and Widow McClintock figured on giving John a good old-fashioned bringing up without any pomp and circumstance —which she might very well have afforded, for her oil income was reaching fabulous proportions. No such monkey-business for Widow McClintock, however: John was taught to work for a living, and know the value of a hard-earned dollar—he was a husky, well-built, fair-haired boy and drove a wagon, and he made a good job of it.

John Steele was teased by his companions because of his shyness. One day while climbing a hill with his wagon loaded with oil, the endboard dropped out and five barrels of crude wabbled over the steep bank. John seethed, and his fellow workers looked for an outburst this time. Collecting himself, he remarked with enforced calmness, "Boys, it's no use trying to do justice to this occasion." John did not smoke or drink or gamble, although he had been known to say damn. No sissy, he could fight—and lick most anybody his equal. Altogether, Widow McClintock appeared to have made a good job of her charge.

Fate decreed that Widow McClintock was to make history. She needed to hurry up the fire in her kitchen stove one morning and poured kerosene on the flames.

A major explosion resulted, flaming oil spewed over her coarse clothing, and she burned to death. Her funeral was Number One which can be laid to the fatal oil can. Her grandson, John Steele, hastened home when the news of the dreadful event was brought to him, ransacked the house, and found some $200,000 which the old lady had hoarded. Inasmuch as John hadn't reached "age," a guardian was appointed, and the boy was allowed a reasonable income.

On his twenty-first birthday, John W. Steele was handed a lump sum of $300,000 and an income of about $2,800 a day. He decided to quit teaming and go see the world. This was doubtless a natural inclination. But suddenly John Steele turned into a three-ring circus.

John went to Philadelphia, and before long he was ordering champagne by dozen baskets and treating theatrical companies to wine suppers. To a Negro comedian who pleased him, he handed a thousand-dollar stickpin. Ballet girls captivated his interest and there were some tall doings. John W. Gaylord, an artist in burnt cork and member of one troupe of actors, furnishes these details:

"Yes, John Steele was my particular friend in his palmiest days. I was his room-mate when he cut the shines that celebrated him as the most eccentric millionaire on earth. I was with the Skiff & Gaylord minstrels. Johnnie saw us perform in Philadelphia, got stuck on the business and bought one-third interest in the show. His first move was to get $5,000 worth of woodcuts at his own expense; they were all the way from a one-sheet to a twenty-four-sheet in size and the largest amount any concern had ever owned. The cartoon which attracted so much attention, 'Bring That Skiff Over Here,' was in the lot. We went on the road, did a monsterous business everywhere, turned people away, and were prosperous.

"Reaching Utica, N. Y., Johnnie treated to a supper for the company, which cost $1,000. He then conceived the idea of travelling by his own train and purchased an engine, a sleeper and a baggage car. Dates for two weeks were cancelled and we went junketing, Johnnie footing the bills. At Erie we had a $500 supper; and so it went. It was here that Johnnie bought his first hack. After a short ride he presented it to the driver. Our dates being cancelled, Johnnie insisted on indemnifying us for the loss of time. He paid all salaries, estimated the probable business receipts upon the basis of packed houses and paid that also to our treasurer.

"In Chicago he gave another exhibition of his eccentric traits. He leased the Academy of Music for the season and we did a big business. Finally he proposed a benefit for Skiff & Gaylord and sent over to rent the Crosby Opera House, then the finest in the country. The manager sent back the insolent reply; 'We won't rent our house to an infernal nigger show.' Johnnie got warm under the collar. He went down to their office in Root & Cady's music store.

" 'What will you take for your house and sell it outright?' he asked Mr. Root.

" 'I don't want to sell.'

" 'I'll give you a liberal price. Money is no object.'

"Then Johnnie pulled out a roll from his valise, counted out $200,000 and asked Root if that was an object. Mr. Root was thunderstruck. 'If you are that kind of a man you can have the house for the benefit free of charge.' The benefit was the biggest success ever known in minstrelry. The receipts were $4,500 and more were turned away than could be given admission. Next day Johnnie hunted up one of the finest carriage horses in the city and presented it to Mr. Root for the courtesy extended.

"Oh, Johnnie was a prince with his money. I have seen him spend as high as one hundred thousand dollars in one day. That was the time he hired the Continental Hotel in Philadelphia and wanted to buy the Girard House. He went to the Continental and politely said to the clerk: 'Will you please tell the proprietor that J. W. Steele wishes to see him?' 'No sir,' said the clerk; 'the landlord is busy.' Johnnie suggested he could make it pay the clerk to accommodate the whim. The clerk became disdainful and Johnnie tossed a bell-boy a twenty dollar gold piece with the request. The result was an interview with the landlord. Johnnie claimed he had been ill-treated and requested the dismissal of the clerk. The proprietor refused and Johnnie offered to buy the hotel. The man said he could not sell, because he was not the entire owner. A bargain was made to lease it one day for $8,000. The cash was paid over and Johnnie installed as landlord. He made me bell-boy, while Slocum officiated as clerk. The doors were thrown open and every guest in the house had his fill of wine and edibles free of charge. A huge placard was posted in front of the hotel: 'OPEN HOUSE TODAY: EVERYTHING FREE, ALL ARE WELCOME.' It was a merry lark. The whole city seemed to catch on and the house was full. When Johnnie thought he had fun enough he turned the hostelry over to the landlord, who reinstated the odious clerk. Here was a how-de-do. Johnnie was frantic with rage. He went over to the Girard and tried to buy it. He arranged with the proprietor to 'buck' the Continental by making the prices so low that everybody would come there. The Continental did mighty little business so long as the arrangement lasted.

"The day of the hotel transaction we were up at Arch Street. A rain setting in, Johnnie approached a hack in front of a fashionable store and tried to engage it to carry us up to the Girard. The driver said it was impossible, as he had a party in the store. Johnnie tossed him a five hundred dollar bill and the hackman said he would risk it. When we arrived at the hotel, Johnnie said: 'See here, Cabby, you are a likely fellow. How would you like to own that rig?' The driver thought he was joking, but Johnnie handed him $2,000. A half-hour later the delighted driver returned with the statement that the purchase had been effected. Johnnie gave him $1,000 more to buy a stable and that man today is the wealthiest hack-owner in Philadelphia."

Johnnie Steele won the name of "Coal Oil Johnnie." Of all the characters of the oil-boom days, doubtless his escapades stand out foremost—although he was not always as silly as he has been pictured. He did many good things, showering money here and there where it bore fruit, and once presented the city of Franklin with a white marble monument for her Civil War dead. That monument, by the way, was paid for out of one day's income of Coal Oil Johnnie's fabulous wealth.

A few big deals flopped and before long Coal Oil

Johnnie was on the toboggan slide, landing in a heap of debt which included a bill of $20,000 to the Girard House in Philadelphia, $10,000 lawyer fees, $5,000 to a jeweler, $2,000 for liquors, $2,000 for an oil painting, $300 for hats—all in all the grand total was somewhere near $35,000. Assets: fond memories. He died at Fort Crook, Nebraska, where he had been working as a station agent on the C. B. & Q. in late December, 1920. One of his last public utterances was this:

"You bet I had a good time while it lasted. I would only be worrying if I had all that money now. I'm enjoyin' life and feelin' fine—buyin' beer instead of wine. What's the difference?"

CHAPTER EIGHTEEN

THESE two newspaper "notices" were run in the river news column of the Pittsburgh *Commercial* on the last day of February, 1866:

"HO FOR THE GOLD FIELDS OF IDAHO.—The new and magnificent steamer Peter Balen, Capt. John A. Williamson, is rapidly reaching completion. We have seen several boats in our time, but the present one exceeds anything in the steamboat way we have seen. She is certainly a curiosity, and well worth a visit. She has been fitted out without regard to expense, and does credit to all concerned in getting her up. Capt. Williamson may justly feel proud of his boat."

"HO FOR THE ALLEGHENY OIL REGIONS.—The splendid passenger steamer Peerless, Capt. A. D· Russell, leaves this day for Oil City and intermediate points. This boat is new, and was built expressly for this trade. She has been fitted out in a superior manner. She has fine speed and excellent accommodations. The first clerk is Mr. J. K. Caldwell, an officer who will see that passengers have the best of attention. She is now at the foot of Irwin Street."

I have included both of the notices because I believe they are interesting; not because I propose to talk about them—for that is not my intention. They indicate that young men with ambitions to "go places" had places to go in 1866—these advance notices have an enticing allure about them, and it would be difficult to choose between them—much would depend on whether you would prefer having your gold served up to you in solid form or in liquid form—fortunes either place, for the asking—Idaho or Oil City.

What the notices did not say, and which will soon register protest in its own behalf, is the cargo this super-duper *Peerless* proposes to smother herself with on the upbound Allegheny voyage. She will have an assortment of horses and mules on her main deck, pawing and stomping and braying, and she will have empty oil barrels piled over her boiler deck, and on the roof. She will reek of mules, horses, and oil—but the passengers will not mind that at all; most of them won't, anyhow, because they will expect such things, and come prepared to while their time away by drinking whisky and raising general Cain. The odors issuing from the pack of humanity which will engage passage aboard the *Peerless* will doubtless be superior garbage; the mules and horses are the ones which are deserving of commiseration.

During the high tide of the oil excitement, one person estimated that fully twelve thousand horses were engaged in the transportation of oil from one place to another; usually from the wells to the railroads or

the river. Great numbers of mules were also used; how many, exactly, this compiler of statistics did not say —likely he didn't know; we must guess at this assumption; he didn't say he didn't know; he didn't say anything about how many mules—fact is, he didn't even mention a mule—not a single one, while listing his statistics—yet pretty soon he fetches up out of a blue sky and drags down a mule every time he needs one in his story; but this method is an old one, dating back to Genesis, so he is following a strict precedent—but still I can't tell you how many mules were used in the Allegheny country.

One thing certain, and you can lay it down as a fact, that more mules and horses were misused than used. The treatment they got was frightful—barbarous —murderous. The roads were something like the Mississippi River on a small scale; each one a nonflowing stream anywhere from six to ten feet deep and filled with a goo from shore to shore which, being a mixture of crude oil and clay, was one of the stickiest mixtures ever concocted. Many horses and mules had not a hair below their eyes—eaten away by this viscous paste— raw, sore, and bleeding. An Oil Creek teamster, rubber-booted to the waist and flannel-shirted to the chin, was savage with the use of the whip. Transportation was what he required, and it was cheaper to rawhide a horse or mule to death than to try to cure it; and his objective was simply to get all the work out of an animal that was in it before it keeled over and gave a last merciful gasp and closed its eyes for the last time—

usually to sink out of sight in the quagmire, thus not presenting any burial problems.

Another major job for horses was that of dragging empty oil boats up Oil Creek for loading. This was done while the water was at a fair boating stage, usually in the cold months of the year. Slush or ice and floating oil shaved the hair off the poor creatures as if done with a razor. The treatment of the patient creatures—thousands were literally murdered—was frightful and few survived. For them the plea of inability availed nothing. They were worked until they dropped dead. As a single trip realized such handsome profit, these brutal drivers scarce felt the financial loss.

If there is any lurking doubt as to the veracity of these statements, suffice it to say the last several paragraphs came almost word for word from the pen of a man who was on the ground all the while and witnessed these things.

This recital of man's inhumanity to animals reminds me that a short time ago there appeared in the *Reader's Digest* several stories by Carl Sandburg, lifted from his *Abraham Lincoln: The War Years.* Among them was this one:

"The President, glancing about the telegraph hut, noticed three tiny kittens wandering, mewing as if lost. He picked one up and asked it, 'Where is your mother?' Someone answer, 'The mother is dead.'

"As he petted the little one: 'Then she can't grieve as many a poor mother is grieving for a son lost in battle.' Gathering the two others in his hands, he put them on his lap, stroked their fur, and according to Admiral Porter, meditated: 'Kitties, thank God you are cats, and can't understand this terrible strife that is going on.' And to Bowers, 'Colonel, I hope you will see that these poor little motherless waifs are given plenty of milk and treated kindly.'

"Several times later Horace Porter noticed Lincoln fondling these kittens. 'He would smooth their coats and listen to them purring their gratitude to him.' A curious sight it was, thought Porter, 'at an army headquarters, upon the eve of a great military crisis in the nation's history, to see the hand which had affixed the signature to the Emancipation Proclamation and had signed the commissions from the general-in-chief to the lowest lieutenant tenderly caressing three stray kittens.' "

In late March, 1865, a man named Booth stroked a cat at Franklin, Pennsylvania, up the Allegheny River. This Booth was a queer fellow, and frequently harbored stray cats, and gave them saucers of milk when they mewed for it. Moreover, he had a passionate love for animals of most any sort—and also in late March, 1865, he is recorded as having been aboard a ferryboat crossing the river at Franklin when some inhuman whelp threw a fine setter into the river. The poor beast swam to the rear of the ferry and Booth pulled him in. He caressed the dog and bitterly denounced the fellow who had done the act. Upon another occasion he knocked down a teamster whom he caught beating a horse that was unable to pull a heavy load out of a mudhole. Queer fellow, this Booth; an actor fellow—owned a well which was pumping about twenty barrels a day over on the Fuller Farm, fronting on the Allegheny River. One morning in early April, he left Franklin, saying he would "be gone east" several days. He carried only a satchel, which indicated he did not expect to be gone long—everything else was left intact in his rooms at Franklin. Nothing was heard of him until telegraph wires hummed the news of Abraham Lincoln's death—Franklin was electrified, for the assassin was this fellow Booth—John Wilkes Booth.

CHAPTER NINETEEN

It is one thing to own an oil well producing 800 barrels daily; it is another thing to get these 800 barrels to market. In 1859 the total oil production in the Pennsylvania regions amounted to 1,873 barrels. In 1861—just two years later—the production ran to 2,119,045 barrels. All the cooperage plants this side of Christendom working on a 24-hour schedule, including Sundays and holidays, couldn't have knocked out two million barrels in 1861. Today things are different, and Henry Ford can pat an airplane and murmur, "Yes, fifty thousand of these a year." Such mass production didn't extend to the barrel industry in Civil War times. Why, a barrel was a thing that had to be built—can't fool a barrel together, for the danged thing will leak—you've got to have the oak just so, and the hoops just so, and the heads just so—else you've got no barrel at all; you've delivered yourself a sprinkling can.

A man drilling an oil well cannot predict how many barrels he is going to need—perhaps none at all. Usually some nominal number of them. Frequently, up in the Allegheny regions, the drillers would work for months and months, anticipating the "oil sand," and get nothing —then they would become discouraged, and feel like quitting, but some other fellow had struck a fair flow just ten feet deeper, so they would take heart again and plug along and whack the tools down deeper, and spend money like water. Still nothing—perhaps some salt water. A little deeper. No, dry hole. No luck at all. To hell with the oil well; let the morning-glories have it. Charge it off to profit and loss—red ink; dry hole. Then, in the middle of the night, with nobody around at all—WHOOSH! A roar that could be heard for miles, and a black stream of spray blowing upward for a hundred feet or so. "She's come in! She's a winner!" Some devil-may-care idiot contracts to "cap" the well for $500—and does it, perhaps—but more often he doesn't, and creeks of the precious liquid flow down ravines and hillsides.

"Build earth dams!" Shovels are brought, and brigades of men try to stop the runaway oil. Large ponds of the liquid are captured. "Barrels! Barrels! Barrels!" A futile cry—for there are no barrels, at least not near enough to care for the emergency.

Countless thousands of gallons of such "wildcat" oil were saved, thanks to the Allegheny River. Small timber barges, known as "bulkboats," were constructed; each one a fairly safe reservoir for 600 barrels or so. Scores of these bulk boats were rushed to the scene when a gusher was ushered in. Pipe lines were hastily laid—"Take it away! Take it away!" More important than a squabble about prices was the mere fact of getting rid of the surplus. Oil to burn, and money to burn—the whole show seems so ridiculously absurd that I present here a factual example:

In April, 1863, Sam Fertig went up Oil Creek to deepen an abandoned well which had proved a "dry hole." Early in May he encountered a crevice at 450 feet. Fearing to lose his tools, Fertig shut down until he could consult with the owners. This delay held operations up for about two weeks, and meanwhile surface water had about filled the hole. The owners decided to let Fertig continue his operation, so on May 15, in the afternoon, everything was ready. "Start her slowly," Noble (an owner) shouted from the derrick to Fertig, who stood beside the engine and turned on the steam. The rods moved up and down with a steady stroke, bringing a stream of fresh water, which it was hoped a day's pumping might exhaust. There was much anxiety —inasmuch as the owners had just turned down an offer of $100,000 for half-interest in the well.

Noble went to an eating house nearby for lunch. He was munching a sandwich when a boy in the door bawled, "Golly! Ain't that well spoutin' oil?"

Turning around, Noble saw a column of oil and water spewing a hundred feet, enveloping the trees and the derrick in dense spray. The gas roared, the ground fairly shook, and the workmen hastened to extinguish the fire beneath the boiler. The "Noble" well, destined to be the most profitable ever known, had begun its dazzling career at a dizzy figure of 3,000 barrels a day.

Crude was $4 a barrel, rose to $6, to $7—to $13. Compute the receipts from the Noble well at these quotations—$12,000 at first and then $39,000 a day.

Soon the foaming volume filled the hollow close to the well and ran into the creek. What was to be done? For $200 three men crawled through the blinding shower and contrived to attach a stop-cock device to the pipe. By sunset a 700-barrel tank was overflowing. Boatmen down the creek, notified to come at once for all they wanted at $2 a barrel, by midnight took oil directly from the well. Next morning the stream was turned in a 3,000-barrel tank, filling it in 21 hours. Sixty-two thousand barrels were shipped and 15,000 tanked, exclusive of leakage and waste, in thirty days. Week after week the flow continued, declining to 600 barrels a day in eighteen months.

The production of this gusher—over 700,000 barrels—netted upward of $4,000,000. Little wonder sensible persons did odd and foolish things. I have said that wells were drilled in graveyards sometimes: the first man to die at Oil City after the oil excitement happened to be a Negro, and he was buried in a lot on the flats. Somebody wanted that precise spot the next day to drill a well and the corpse was planted on the hillside. The next week that particular location was selected for a well and the body was again exhumed. To be sure of getting the deceased out of reach of the drill, the friends boated the remains down the river to Butler County. Twelve years later Mr. Deadman was again disturbed—an oil company leased the old graveyard—and this time the son of the deceased brought his daddy's remains home and planted him in the garden; just in case. . . .

But, getting back to the oil-barrel problem for a moment: these bulkboats were nothing more than small wooden flatboats and oil was pumped directly into them. Getting these affairs down the river was as ticklish a proposition as trying to carry a brimful plate of soup from the kitchen to the dining room without losing cargo. Any jolt, such as grounding on a bar, would cause the oil to rush toward the focus of the impact and slop overboard, and often a bulkboat capsized, losing all. A system of partitions, or bulkheads, was built into later bulkboats with varying success, and the tops were decked over—these pioneer attempts being the progenitors of the modern "tank barge" which hauls perhaps 1,200 tons of oil or gasoline at a single loading. The haulage of petroleum products, by the way, recently has sprung up to third place in point of tonnage prominence on the Allegheny-Ohio River system, being dominated only by coal and sand-and-gravel.

That spouting bonanza, the Noble well, was drilled in Oil Creek valley, about eleven miles above the mouth of the stream. Oil Creek, in its natural state, is not deep enough to float an 18-foot skiff except when draining off a freshet at odd intervals. It wriggles down a narrow ravine and bubbles a minor contribution into the Allegheny River at Oil City. The enormous production of the Noble gusher, as well as that of a horde of others along the creek, presented a critical problem of transportation. The mud roads were worse than useless. The scheme of a major system of pipe lines was a dream which had not yet materialized. The gushers were gushing: the oil *had* to move. The plan adopted by these sons-of-greasedom was a novel one.

An artificial reservoir dam was built at the headwaters of Oil Creek near the spot where Drake's original well came in. Water was impounded there. Horses and mules were hitched to empty oil barges lying in wait at the mouth of the stream and were persecuted into the task of dragging those nondescript craft up the shallow creek bed to the wells. This meant that the animals had to be belly-deep in water most of the way, and in winter months it was a usual sight to see their tails frozen into cakes of ice. The extreme urgency for speed did not allow for rest periods and an animal driven to this task often remained immersed in freezing water from the time he was hitched up at Oil City until, hours later, he had arrived at the destination. Frequently barges were hauled as high as the Noble well, some eleven torturous miles.

Time was allowed for filling the barges with their liquid cargo and, at a prearranged moment, a large hole was opened in the reservoir dam and a torrent of water gushed down the creek, causing a rise of three or four feet. The cry of "Pond freshet!" went up from thousands of throats and frequently as many as two or three hundred craft of all descriptions were turned loose at the mercy of the raging flood. Well drillers, oil-field hands, teamsters, every able-bodied man available, dropped his chores and climbed aboard a boat to help "navigate" it out to Oil City.

The art of navigating these craft consisted of making a herculean attempt to keep them in motion. This meant that the loaded boats frequently rammed the bank, turned end for end, rammed one another, collided with bridge piers, jammed on gravel bars, sank on protruding rocks and otherwise acted like a pile of straws racing pell-mell down a street gutter after a summer shower. On a particular freshet staged in May, 1864, no less than 20,000 barrels of crude were lost in a "jam" on the Oil City bridge pier alone. One of the leading boats caught the stone obstruction broadside, hung there, and the latecomers, unable to halt, piled down upon a general scene of destruction. As many as one thousand men were engaged in these artificial splashes.

"Where in hell is Parker?" became a byword of the region when a pillar of the Presbyterian Church raced to the bank of Oil Creek to find his loaded boat lying there unmanned and the creek rising at a rapid rate. Parker was his hired navigator. Parker was not there.

During the oil heyday some 2,000 craft of all description were used in petroleum transportation on the Allegheny River. The "guiper," scow-shaped and holding 25 to 50 barrels, was the smallest. The "French Creekers" held 1,000 to 1,200 barrels and could accommodate their cargo either in bulk or in barrel. Oil was shipped in bulk when prices were low; when prices bettered, barrels were used, as the usual rule, to reduce leakage and attendant loss. Oftentimes thousands of barrels—new ones, and empty—were lashed together like a raft and floated down from Olean, New York.

These guipers and French Creekers and flats and bulkboats were floated out to Pittsburgh when they received their load. The usual method of returning them "empty" to Oil City was to engage a steamboat for the job. Sometimes cargoes of new barrels were delivered up the river this way, piling them in the empty craft en route to the oil fields. When the river was too low for steamboat navigation, the oldtime keelboat held sway.

It took Captain Dan Fry to tell about these things; he, at the age of ninety, had a mind sharp as a tack, and he'd sit down sort of stooped over, and squint his eyes, and wave the index finger of his right hand like a baton, and rattle along, spilling out facts and dates from his card-index memory. To uncork him, and get him fizzing, all a body needed to do was display some genuine interest. Here is how he would go:

"I built a keelboat on the flat across from my place, Clinton, during the early days of the oil boom, got her launched, and took her down to Pittsburgh and put the cargo box on. First trip we loaded her out with about 85 tons of freight and hauled her up to Oleopolis (about eight miles above Oil City) with horses. Called her the *Olive Branch*. We got her unloaded, and dropped back out to Oil City, and found a cargo of oats and mill feed that needed delivering back at Oleopolis—so contracted to do the job for $75. By that time there was a big lot of barreled oil piled up at Oleopolis, and we hustled that on the *Olive Branch* and floated it out to Pittsburgh, and got $705 freight. We made that round trip in fourteen days and got $1,100 clear profit for our trouble. The keelboat cost $1,650 in the first place, and Stoffel Walthower came along then and said he wanted the *Olive Branch* most awful bad, and I said, 'Bad enough to pay $1,650 for it?' and he said he did, so we made a deal right there and then.

"Then I got hold of a big guiper called the *Elephant*—she was a dandy; had good quarters for the crew, and bedding, and everything a body'd need and then some. We loaded her up with 3,000 empty oil barrels at Pittsburgh and got Bill Munhall to tow us up to Oil City with his steamboat *Brilliant*. I got thirty cents apiece out of those barrels. Then we loaded the *Elephant* up with 300 barrels of crude and dropped her back out to Pittsburgh—got sixty cents a barrel for it. One time I put twenty-eight hundred bushels of coal on the *Elephant* down at Saw Mill Run at Pittsburgh; got it for six-and-a-half cents a bushel and then Bill Munhall towed us up to Tidioute. Mr. Myers, one of the Economites (they had a big tract across the river there—got it on some sort of a foreclosure) offered me a dollar a bushel for the coal. He said he'd be back to the boat at one o'clock with the money. I said I'd wait until then. While I was sitting and waiting a fellow came over from the Cornplanter Oil Company and offered me $1.25 a bushel. I told him to sit down and take it easy, and kept watching the time, and presently one o'clock came and no Mr. Myers. 'She's yours, at a dollar-and-a-quarter,' I told the Cornplanter fellow. Oh, coal in the upper end of the Allegheny was worth a good deal those days, with all the drilling going on. I sold that old *Elephant* to Andy Brunner for $900 cash one day—paid $600 for her in the first place."

CHAPTER TWENTY

CAPTAIN DAN FRY was a little fellow who, if he were found under a Christmas tree, would pass for Santa Claus dressed up in store clothes. Same twinkly eyes, ruddy cheeks, perky nose, beard and all. He showed up every year at the annual meeting of the Allegheny River Boatmen's Association and was the center of the scene. He always was called upon to make a speech.

Captain Fry would slowly get to his feet and take a good, long lingering look all around the hall until silence reigned supreme. Then, in a quiet, almost unhearable voice, he would say, "Mr. Chairman of the meeting and my friends of the Allegheny River, the most noble stream in the world." Another pause. Captain Fry's merry eyes roved around until he discovered a particular face in the audience which suited him. Thereafter all remarks were directed to that individual. "I am not much of a speechmaker, but . . ." he said. His story usually picked up a thread of the long and adventurous life he had spent keelboating and steamboating on his beloved river.

The homely little reunions of this Boatmen's Association started back in 1897 and met annually, without interruption, until 1919. Each one had a new tinge of sadness, inasmuch as the members were growing old, and tragedy stalked in all eyes when a new arrival announced, "No, Jim can't get here today: he's down with rheumatism bad and can't make it." To men who have lived a river life an inability to gather among old friends and rehearse the glories of a past yesteryear is worse than the inevitable visit of the Grim Reaper in person. "Jim can't get down today." Real trouble, there. Heads would shake, canes would pound the sidewalk in mute appeal, and tears would come. "Jim can't get down, did you hear?"

A whole year has rolled around since any one of those veterans has seen Jim. No word, no sign. Christmas has come and gone without the exchange of a post-card greeting. Yet Jim belongs at the meeting of the Boatmen's Association. Jim is one of the fellows. Rivermen, as a group, are an odd lot in this respect: those bitter tears were springing from a knowledge of how Jim felt about it—laid up at home with that persecuting, damnable, inhuman failing of old age: rheumatism. Each old-timer could see Jim sitting at a window looking out on the valley and aching his heart out to be at "the meeting."

Lumbermen, rivermen, and raftsmen frequently are depicted as being a degenerate lot. Carousing, yelping, swearing, drinking, fighting—uneducated, slothful, indolent (except in emergencies), and devoid of Christian principles generally. To deny these assumptions would be ridiculous; yet to swallow them hook, line, and sinker is equally wrong. There is a spontaneous fraternal bond which knits them into a big family.

At one of the annual meetings, Captain Fry had been called upon, and had gone through his usual rigmarole of preliminaries, and then he launched off into a story of how he had gone to work on the keelboat *Great Western* plying between Pittsburgh and Tionesta back in '54. When the current got too swift for poling, the heavy boat was propelled upstream by horses. Frequently from ten to thirty-five tons of merchandise was taken up the Allegheny this way. Captain Fry's job was to manage the animals from the shore, where long towropes hitched back to the keelboat. Passengers were transported on this glorified canalboat. Bunks were provided for the women travelers, veiled off by flimsy and makeshift curtains. Then men slept on the floor. The venerable captain was relating this portion of his recollections when a feminine voice piped up in the audience to exclaim, "My goodness! How did you men sleep?" With a Kris Kringle gleam in his merry eyes, Captain Fry replied, "Why—why—we slept with our eyes shut."

On the Ohio and Mississippi River system, most of the impossible tasks were accomplished by youngsters in their teens or early twenties. Examples are legion: for instance, the largest steamboat built for the Mississippi River was owned and captained by a Louisville youth, Captain Ed Sturgeon—his audacity was the talk of the times and his boat, the *Eclipse*, was the fastest thing ever built for rivers. During the Civil War, one of the prominent gunboats was named *Queen of the*

West—she was continually in the news—doing adventuresome jobs; first to run the batteries at Vicksburg, a feat which was held by many wise heads as sheer impossibility. Her commander: Colonel C. R. Ellet. His age: about nineteen. Captain Dan Fry was in his teens when he rode horseback along the banks of the Allegheny, urging the *Great Western* through swift riffles.

A riverman comes to be a riverman without much fanfare. Within the past month I watched this interesting metamorphosis lay hold on a lad of high school age. He was sitting on the river bank watching a steamboat go by. Some peculiar combination of his attention and attitude and a positive knowledge of the transformation came to me. So swift; so silent! My heart cried out to him, but words did not come. Oh, youth! Oh, my boy; you—right now—are a part of that flowing stream. It has enmeshed you while you sit placidly on a log: that stillness of your body! What is going on in your head? Who knows? You gaze at a collection of boards, paint, sheet iron, and ropes. You see sooty smoke—smoke that you have seen roll from a thousand chimney tops in the same identical way. You hear men shout, as you always have heard men shout. You see reflections of white woodwork in the green river water. You hear the roar of hissing steam. All prosaic and common in your experience until right now as you sit there on a log. Still and tense you sit—but the magic combination is before you; it is the key which has just unlocked something deeper than any man has ever explored. From this day forth you will thrill to the sight of a steamboat. Smoke rolling from high river chimneys will make you ache and want to cry, and sweaty men with tarred ropes in their hands will be gods to you!

The "western river" boatman, whether he makes his living on the Allegheny, or the Ohio, or the Mississippi, has come through some such experience as this, and is pretty much the same fellow. More accurately he belongs to a similar group of fellows—for there is no single "composite" riverman who will be a gauge stick for his clan.

There was Captain W. K. Hudson who lived at Clinton. He was in his eighties when I knew him back in my high school days. He picked many of the cobblestones out of the Allegheny and boated them down to Pittsburgh for making the Monongahela wharf—how long ago? A few scribbled figures and some subtraction brings the date to 1850 or thereabouts. His snowy crop of unruly hair and flowing beard was in view at every Allegheny Boatmen's meeting. One time I tackled him about the "good old days."

"Say, boy," he said, "are you old enough to go to war?"

This was barely two months before the Armistice of 1918. "No," I said, "not quite—but how about the days when you were captain on the *Cornplanter* and the *Clara Fisher*, away before the days of the oil excitement?"

"Ever farm any?" he countered.

I admitted growing up with hayfields, a barn, four or five horses, and a few pet geese.

"I had a war farm this summer," he declared, with triumph in his voice. "Raised some of the dangedest biggest beans you ever laid your eyes on, and potatoes—say! Why don't you come on down to my place tonight and let me show you?"

A blank notebook in my hand looked bleak. The sharpened pencil in my other tapped with nervous impatience. I wanted a story for our river paper, the *Waterways Journal.* Maybe if I would explain to Captain Hudson about it—"I'd surely like to have a story about some of your adventures for the paper."

"I declare," laughed the aged skipper, "you don't mean to tell me anybody'd want to print what would come rattlin' out of my head? Newspapers are too full of war these times. What we need is to encourage those boys of ours over there in France; write something along that line, why don't you?"

An inspiration shot through my system. "Maybe you could tell me something," I ventured.

"I wasn't in any war," he said quietly. "Nearest I ever came to getting shot was away up here on the Allegheny at Red House Shoals. Ever hear of that place: up near the New York State line? A couple of us was pushing a keelboat up the river and the day got almighty hot so we laid over a spell to get our wind. Another fellow and me decided we'd take a skiff and row on up to the big island just above us and do some fishing. That's the best place for bass you can find along the river—along where the state line goes across. We didn't remember about being up in the Indian reservation, and about the time we got our bait on the hooks and had the lines set, we heard a whoop! and looked up and here come a whole drove of Injuns with murder in their eyes. It come to us like a flash that we was poaching on their territory so I took one meaningful look at my partner and dove in the river, clothes and all, and took out for the main shore. My partner yelled, 'I can't swim! Don't leave me here!' and he waded out on the bar until the water was up around his middle, but I was hauling up on the far side by that time and was out of reach. Those Injuns started in the water after my partner and he seen it was either sink or swim or Lord knows what, but he was deathly afraid of water, so he turned around and clasped his hands like he was prayin' and says, 'Oh, please, Mr. Injuns, don't kill me; I didn't mean no harm!' Them Injuns stood there thunderstruck like they never seen such a sight as that before. Presently one big feller looks at the rest of them, shrugs his shoulders and says, 'Ugh!' and they turned around and tracked away again. My partner turns to me and yells, 'I'm saved!' I says yes, you're saved but the skiff's floated off. And so it had. I had to swim down the river and overhaul the boat and row it clean back up to the island and rescue him."

Captain Hudson looked toward the Allegheny, then he looked at me. "Not much of a hero, am I?" he said, abashed. He added, "That would be an awful thing to tell the boys in France—that's why I stick to a war farm; can do my bit that way. Raise big beans, and potatoes; that farm land down our way is just suited for such business. Can't you come down and look 'er over tonight?"

Religion and a riverman are inseparable, strange as it may seem. Captain Lewis Pope never ran his boat on a Sunday; sure as Saturday midnight came, he'd blow a toot on the whistle and hunt out a good big sycamore tree and tie up until Monday morning, no matter where he was. Captain Jim Wood had just as much religion as that, but he was in the coal business and had to barge his "black diamonds" out on the freshets: laying over on a Sunday would mean that the water would get away from him and he'd be left stranded and all his competitors would sell their coal. So he had an organ installed in his steamboat, and every Sunday noon there was a service, and everybody from potato peeler to the dandified pilot, and including the hell-roaring Irish mate, had to come in and sing "Rock of Ages" and hear some Scripture and bow his head in prayer. Captain Jim was his own preacher; always led the services. Old Bill Whipple told me about these things; Bill was a good deck hand in his day.

Bill said this about Captain Jim Wood:

"One Sunday we were just finishing up with the service and somebody yelled up the front steps that a barge of coal had got loose from the tow. Captain Jim shut the Big Book, said 'Amen,' and took out that door with the awfulest, most blood-curdling cussing you ever heard in your life."

Cursing is an art that bears cultivation, and the Allegheny River came in for its share. One youngster started in as a raft hand and it was said of him that he "was the most awkward swearer on the river." But he persevered, and one day became proficient. An old lady was sitting on the steamboat's boiler deck one summer afternoon while this gentleman was urging an unruly cow down the stageplank. Nothing went right. The cow sat down. The bull rails slipped and went into the river. An offshore breeze blew the boat around and the heel of the gangplank nearly fell over the edge of the forecastle. The situation became intolerable. Unmindful of the dear old lady's presence, the irate riverman started in softly, gained in volume, erupted and exploded, came to crescendo, and faded away like a retreating thunderstorm. The cow, hypnotized by this spell of music, got up and walked aboard as placidly as could be. The wind died down. The old lady removed her hand from her heart, blushed to the roots of her hair. Waveringly she arose, leaned over the rail and called, "You, down there!" The riverman looked aloft. He stammered, "I'm sorry, ma'am."

The old lady could only repeat, "What language! What language! Saints protect us, what language!"

In the evening this riverman had a strange request. The little lady asked him, oh! so secretly, would he mind writing down those blasphemous words! She confided that her heart was touched. What she had heard that afternoon was the most honest poetry "told in the liveliest way" she had run onto in her lifetime, she said.

What was said will never be known, for, try as he could, this riverman could not remember the formula. One of the crying shames of literature is that all such honest expression of provocation is deleted. Actually (when expertly done, of course) it easily ranks with the works of the immortals. And the Allegheny River brand would fill Volume One.

A crop of young businessmen began taking interest in the meetings of the Allegheny River Boatmen's Association and, in 1919, a resolution was offered to change the name of the organization to the Allegheny River Improvement Association. Naturally there was some opposition from the gray-hairs in the meeting. Their protests were "talked down" and the more modern title was adopted. The reasoning behind the alteration was sensible enough: the group was changing from an annual "reunion" into a body of alert Allegheny River residents wishing to promote the construction of additional locks and dams up the river, to forward the flood control project, and to go on record as favoring the building of a canal linking Lake Erie with Pittsburgh via French Creek and the Allegheny River.

The old fellows came to the meetings of the "new" association and listened to the crusading orations with respectful attention. Once in a while some veteran like S. A. Phillips of Foxburg would rise from his seat, pound his cane, and interrupt a flow of rhetoric. "Excuse me, please, but you were listing the natural resources of the valley; now you did a fair job of it, but you left out one or two of the most important ones.

Mr. Speaker, you are too young a man to remember when we boated fire brick out from Red Bank Creek to Pittsburgh. I would like to state that you should never forget clay when you are making a list of the natural resources of this valley. That clay up Red Bank Creek is the *best in the world*, and many a barge of it I've steered out to Pittsburgh, and when we'd get to the city, there'd be piles and piles of pig metal, and railroad iron, and lumber and staves, and hay, reaching all the way from Hand Street bridge down to the Point, and all of it had just come down the Allegheny. And ice, too; there used to be a lot of ice shipped . . ."

The chairman would squirm, look perplexed and uneasy, and eventually rap for order and cause Mr. Phillips to sit down, and allow the "Mr. Speaker" to proceed with his declarations and declamations about what ought to be done.

The meeting of the Improvement Association went rather lame in the fall of 1940. A good bit of the spice and zest of the gatherings withered away as the old-timers, those true-sons-of-the-Allegheny, vanished.

CHAPTER TWENTY-ONE

NITROGLYCERIN is as innocent looking as lard oil and was used for some time, before its violent explosive properties were known, as a homeopathic remedy for headache, because a few drops of the liquid rubbed on any portion of the body resulted in an acute headache for the patient. Had said patient an inkling of this medicine—phew! He might also have had a case of jitters! Once in a while some dunderhead took a swig of nitroglycerin—mistaking it for whisky, usually—and ended up very dead. Hence this "headache remedy" was labeled POISON. One day a consignment of this peculiar medicine exploded on a New York street, and caused some havoc. Newspapers "wondered" about this explosion and some scientists "investigated." Only then did the explosive quality of the fluid reveal itself and the world came to know that fuming nitric acid, sulphuric acid, and glycerin mixed in certain proportions was the recipe for an artificial earthquake.

Nitroglycerin soon became a commonplace in the Allegheny valley. Tin tubes, called "torpedoes," loaded with the stuff, were carefully lowered into oil wells that were "ailing," and discharged by concussion. The sick well, which may have been clogged with paraffin, or anemic and listless on some reason of its own account, usually took a surprising recovery when this subterranean shot went off in its anatomy. Often a well so treated "came back to life" and was a thing of animation and interesting production for years after.

This shows how powerful nitroglycerin is: a big fellow walked into a blacksmith shop at Modoc, up Allegheny valley, one day, and asked for work. Asked how strong he was, the stranger bulged his muscles and claimed he could strike an anvil harder than any mortal alive or dead. The owner of the smithy—one Bob Wilson—decided to have some fun. Wilson poured one or two drops of what looked like lard oil on his anvil, gave the stranger a sledge, and said, "Demonstrate." The stranger, wishing to make a permanent impression, lammed down with the sledge with all that was in him and hit the anvil one terrible wallop: the sledge soared through the roof and the "superman" went out the side of the smithy, taking planks, two-by-fours, and three joists with him. "You'll do," said Wilson, "report for work in the morning."

Bill Myers, over in Bradford, claims he worked around a nitroglycerin factory and got his shoe soles soaked with it. Coming out of the building, he inadvertently stomped a stone, and sailed heavenward. Returning to earth, he lit on his other foot and began a second ascension He felt stiff and sore for a week or so, but didn't lose any time from work. Nearly everybody who inhabited the Allegheny regions from the latter sixties through the turn of the century had some experience with a "glis-cer-een" explosion.

Charlie Rust had a spat with his wife one morning, slammed the front door when he left for work, vowing he would never return—this up around Bradford. Rust was due to torpedo a well at Sawyer City that morning. The usual crowd of curious spectators had arrived to watch proceedings as Charlie, seething with his domestic troubles, filled a shell, fixed the firing head. For some reason he struck the cap two sharp blows with his hand. Ker—wham! The derrick flew to splinters. A worker named Crouse got a piece of jagged board square between his eyes, which passed clear through his skull; every shred of clothing was stripped from his body. Two other workers were mangled beyond recognition. Rust lit two hundred yards away, battered to a pulp, minus legs, most of his head, and all his clothing. A boy walking to school near by was struck with a section of the derrick, disemboweled, and died in three hours. Six or seven others had miraculous escapes. This catastrophe is singled out from forty or fifty such calamitous affairs because of the possibility that Charlie Rust may have done away with himself purposely—nobody knows but plenty have wondered about it.

Quite a few of the accidents resulting from nitroglycerin explosions happened while the liquid was being transported from one place to another. There are plenty enough trees all the way from Warren to East Brady which have held stray buggy wheels, and assorted arms, legs, bits of hair, skin, horsemeat, and unidentifiable remains of such tragedies. One favored way of getting this explosive up and down the valley was to row it in skiffloads. John Jeffersey, an Indian pilot, who lived at Tionesta in his latter days, was aboard a raft of lumber one night in Brady's Bend when he peered into the inky murk upriver and discovered a skiffload of "nitro" floating down toward the raft. Such skiffs were identified with red flags. The skiff was being rowed by two men; neither of them saw the raft until too late! A collision was inevitable! The men in the skiff "sold out" by jumping into the Allegheny—both were drowned. Indian-pilot Jeffersey leaped forward, caught the skiff, warded it off the raft, jumped aboard yelling, "Me got him! Me run it him and tie!" He guided the skiff through the inky blackness and anchored it safely.

One woman, at least, lost her life during this period of explosive violence, Mrs. Andrew Dalrymple. She and her husband, and a twenty-month-old infant, lived on the hillside about half a mile from Tidioute. One morning the Dalrymple house went to kingdom-come, taking most of the windows around Tidioute with it. Mr. Dalrymple was a "moonlighter" by trade; differing from a "moonshiner" in that he bootlegged nitroglycerin, sidestepping certain patents. Neighbors rushed to the scene and found Dalrymple in fragments, one arm in the creek 400 feet from where the home had been located a few moments ago, and the upper half of his body jammed in an engine house near by, the rest of him blown to atoms, doubtless, as nothing definite was located to account for his legs. A feeble cry from the wreckage disclosed the baby, unhurt. Mrs. Dalrymple was there, too, unconscious; she died two hours later. The baby was adopted by a wealthy Tidioute resident, and grew to be a beautiful girl.

Modern scientific inventions and discoveries in the field of explosives brought a charitable halt to this destruction.

CHAPTER TWENTY-TWO

A SMALL stream empties into the Allegheny River a few miles above Oil City, called Pithole Creek. Once in a while some fisherman goes up there to try his luck, and otherwise, aside from a few wheezing wells, the landscape is devoid of interest. Fact is, one time Sand Bar Johnny Zenn and I came down the Allegheny watching for the mouth of this creek, and missed it: so you see, either we were asleep at the switch or else Pithole Creek wasn't any shucks—and, naturally, I incline toward the latter view of things.

We wanted to see Pithole Creek especially—and I was in a froth for several hours after we missed it, grumbling and growling about the stupidity of mapmakers and the indefinite way they have of running inky streaks of lightning into rivers, making them strike into obvious sheer mountainsides where a creek couldn't worm through with the assistance of all the resources of the Dravo Corporation, biggest contracting outfit on the rivers. I feel mapmakers decorate rivers with tributary creeks for the artistic value; although heaven knows what queer quirk in their brain would cause them to find such aesthetic pleasure in imitating magnified putrefaction germs—which have main stems and wavy legs, very river-and-creekish in appearance. A well-made map is one of the most beautiful and satisfying articles in existence; I never see one but what I want to spread it out on the floor and get down and commune with it, and share all the secrets it has to offer, and read the tiny names, and focus the colors and the shapes in my memory—just to treasure them there. And most maps are reliable until they attempt to run a creek into a river. They'll wiggle a little stream over four counties, and put in fifty exact twists and bends, and the moment they approach the major stream it empties into—she whizzes up over mountain peaks, through gullies, over hill and dale, roller-coaster fashion—all laws of gravitation are suspended, every rule of common sense goes into the wastebasket—and that creek will strike the river at some unheard-of place on a sheer bluff eighty feet high where it *must* drain through an eagle's nest and squirt itself with fire-hose pressure even to reach the river. Even if a creek *could* do this, the water would divide into spray and evaporate before it struck the river; you know so—everybody knows so—except a mapmaker. I suppose he doesn't care, but even so, you'd think he would have conscience enough to unload a creek where it belongs, and not get it off at the wrong landing most *every* time. Pithole Creek was not where it was supposed to be; not on our map, at any rate. I know so because when we got there the creek was not there! It was someplace else. Tie that argument and see what it gets you.

Up Pithole Creek, in 1865—along about the first of May—there was a small settlement consisting of three oil wells, one drilling well, and three houses. Ninety days later a city called Pithole graced the landscape, and had sixteen thousand inhabitants and the third largest post office in the state of Pennsylvania. Sixty hotels could not accommodate the guests. There were churches, stores, homes, palaces of sin, gorgeous barrooms, schools. One year later, there was nothing again. Just as though a moving-picture company built a ten-million-dollar set, used it, and tore it all away again. The whole show was as abrupt as that—the crowning madness of the oil boom in the Allegheny valley.

Fabulous Pithole! Built for suckers, and did a land-office business. The "oil bonanza" there was principally fraud and sham on a tremendous scale. Dry wells were "doctored" and "dosed"—in three separate instances the spouting oil came from a tank near by, secretly connected underground to the well. A smart widow sold her farm at treble its value because of "surface indications" she created by emptying a barrel of oil into her spring—and got properly stuck herself when the "sucker" drilled and found the real McCoy; then this dear widow roundly abused the purchaser "for cheatin' a poor lone woman!" A newcomer, in his haste to get into something good, shelled out a thousand dollars for a share in a gusher that yielded him two quarts of oil a day. Teamsters had no trouble earning twenty dollars a day—nor did they have trouble getting rid of it; there were variety shows, music halls with "pretty girl waiters," dance houses, saloons. Many a fine young gentleman not only "wandered" from the straight-and-narrow: he was jerked off that road of virtue—stripped and fleeced of everything he owned, oftentimes his health as well as his wealth.

An author of those days said this: "Many a comely maiden, yielding to the wiles of the betrayer, rounded up in the brothel and the potter's field." Oh, it must have been awful—with such things as that going on: I mean once you get comely maidens yielding to wiles, it's high time to dust up the shotguns and get the vigilantes organized—yet nobody did, seems. Here is some more news: this author *saw* these things: "Many a husband, forgetting the trusting wife and children at home, wandered from the straight path and tasted the forbidden fruit." I am struck dumb and speechless with horror. But let me gather myself together long enough to deliver a last parting shot: "Many a promising life was blighted, many a hopeful career blasted, many a reputation smirched and many a fond heart broken by the pitfalls and temptations of Pithole." After this rhetorical triumph, the account drops the final curtain with this observation: "The half has never been told."

Ten of the leading hotels had interesting names: Bonta House, Danforth, United States, Chase, Tremont, Buckley, Lincoln, Sherman, St. James, American, Northeast, Seneca, Metropolitan, and Pomeroy. The Bonta House was a three-story hotel with a balcony running entirely around the second floor, steamboat boiler-deck fashion, and another balcony on the third floor; the place was said to have cost $80,000. The Tremont burned while still a youngster—barely six months old; the Danforth sold for $16 soon after, somebody wanted the place badly enough to pay that fancy price for the scrap value; the city actually grew soap-bubble fashion and went to kindling while still seemingly getting bigger! Several bad fires cleaned out much of Pithole. The two banks shut up shop when the oil ceased to flow, and the population moved away; not most of the population—ALL of it.

Some twenty years after Pithole's heyday a 30-foot poplar grew from the cellar of the National Hotel, underbrush covered the Metropolitan Theater, a sunken portion of ground marked the site of the Chase House. The Presbyterian church stood vacant, a silenced bell in the belfry, the front door agape, mud-dauber wasps inspecting the eaves, and a dusty Bible open on the pulpit. Briers and bushes ran riot over a score or so of graves—for Pithole had some deaths in its hectic career.

Nowadays it is hard to find the mouth of Pithole Creek, let alone a trace of the city.

CHAPTER TWENTY-THREE

THE mouth of Pithole Creek holds a fascination for river fellows on its own account—aside from the allure of the 1866 city which thrived up the hollow. The old towboat *Iron City* got stuck on a rock reef there in the spring of 1877 and stayed all summer and most of the fall. Her young skipper, Captain Warren Elsey, knew full well that his gravest danger was from dry air and sunshine—not rocks—for his boat was perched handsomely enough and was safe for the time being. The river fell away from the steamboat completely, and her wooden hull dried out. Captain Elsey had boated on the Allegheny long enough to know that, if one of the river's "pop" rises came along and caught his boat's seams gaping, he would have a wreck on his hands. So he directed the construction of a timber dam, some 300 feet long, across the bed of the channel—getting most of his material from an old railroad near by, using the crossties for cribbing. In this artificial pond, the *Iron City* floated peacefully as a goldfish until well along in October, when fall rains set in, and the river came up, and she was liberated. If I were to end the story here, I can see an old steamboat mate named

Jack McDonough—Irish as his name—commence getting red around the neck, and blinking his sharp blue eyes. This *Iron City* story is one of his favorites. Jack is along toward eighty now, his hair as white as the driven snow, and he uses a cane to punctuate his stories—letting it down easy for each comma, and some harder for a semicolon, and giving her a resounding kerwhack for frequent exclamation points.

"*That* ain't the story," he would fume. "The way *you* tell it, sounds like a Presbyterian funeral sermon [whack]. There was two boats mixed up in it, the *Venture* and the *Iron City*. They left Pittsburgh early that spring to go up to Tionesta for some new barges that was built up there. The *Venture* got up to the mouth of Kiski River and sank [whack] and stayed there six [whack] months [whack]. Warren Elsey, bless his departed soul—he was a good man, don't you forget it—was getting as high as five [whack] hundred [whack] dollars a month for piloting on the Allegheny; that man knew more about the rocks and bars up that river than all those other jack-legs and mud turtles that was raised [whack] up in that country, and had ought to have knowed it, but was too thick skulled to do the work right, y'understand. They hated Elsey [whack] because he was a damn furriner—come from Mon-ge-haley River, so he had coal stink on him, and he wasn't good [whack] enough to associate with them fine pine merchants from Parker and Clarion. But Elsey was too smart for them raft-headed sons o'guns [whack, whack, whack]. You know what I seen once? This is a fact, and may God strike me down if it ain't: I seen a feller who was born on a houseboat at Franklin, and drunk Allegheny River water all his life, and waded in it, and boated on it, and come to have a reputation, y'understand—he [whack] give himself the reputation; said he could pilot from Oil City to Pittsburgh with his eyes shut. Hah! I shipped up on the old *Twilight* to go deck-a-neer and this splinterhead was pilot—we both come to her together. There was a sixteen by ninety flat loaded with coal laying in Painter's Landing that had to go to Sharpsburg. I hooked 'er up and be blowed to let go, and up we started. When we got in the Allegheny there was a current runnin' and this pilot commenced hoggin' over to the Allegheny shore—and you know how those bridge piers used to be staggered along up through there, before they straightened them out; well, that looked funny to me, but this gent had a reputation [whack] and was supposed to be an ace [whack] and a reg'lar weasel-on-wheels so I says to myself, 'Guess he knows what he's doin',' but about then she took a sheer on him and went into a houseboat and ladies and kids came poppin' out ascreamin' and bellerin' and just in time, too—for the flat poked up under a gunnel and sunk that houseboat like a lump of lead. Then he backed out and come ahead on her again, and she took a dive the other way, and hit the bridge pier and sunk the coal flat. He rung to back while I was chopping the flat loose, and kept on backing and I'll be struck down if he didn't run the paddlewheel clean out on the shore so we had to lay a nigger line and get free. 'Mon-ge-haley pilots might stink of coal smoke, but if this here is a sample of some of your Allegheny hickory smoke, give me my time and let me pack my duds and get off of here,' I says to him.—But where was we, oh, yes . . .

"The *Iron City* blowed up in the end; did you know that? Elsey wasn't on her then. She got stuck on a gas main along about Herr's Island, and wiggled and jimmed around and finally bust the gas pipe off, and a big belch of gas came aroarin' up out of the river and caught fire from the furnace, and came near roastin' the whole crew. I expect the *Iron City* went to Davy Jones quicker than any steamboat you ever heard about. Her bones laid up along Herr's Island for a good long time after."

Jack McDonough's opinion of Allegheny pilots was warped because he was a native of the Mon-ge-haley, as most boatmen from the Monongahela River pronounce the name of their stream. The boatmen who are native to any western stream are loyal to their river, and clannish. Jack's cane would do service on your head, likely, if you referred to his Monongahela as "the sewer." Down on Kanawha River you can get into trouble quick as lightning by alluding to "that snake country." Any time you would care to see artificial constellations up the Allegheny, say something about "splinterheads" to a riverman with a big fist.

Anybody will tell you that piloting on the Ohio River from Louisville down is apple pie, because the river is wide and handsome, and the bottom is largely sand. As you come upstream from Louisville, the job gets harder; and when you get to the mouth of the Kanawha River the fun is over—for you are then "getting up in the woods" where the channel is crooked and narrow and the rocks are more frequent and jagged. Above Hannibal the difficulties are compounded, and from Brown's Island on into Pittsburgh a pilot knows no rest at all. All right, then—keep on up the Allegheny; which is a continuation of the Ohio River; the lower end where piloting is "easy" compares to the worst conditions an Ohio River pilot knows about; and as for the upper end—you'd do well to take aboard a good "splinterhead" every time.

One of the more dramatic voyages on the Allegheny River was accomplished in fairly recent years under the direction of a slight, sprightly, fun-loving son-of-the-Allegheny named Thomas E. Clark. Captain Tom took a notion that the old river was being neglected, and needed "improving," so he built a boat (a real stern-wheeler) and came down amid a fanfare of newspaper publicity. Although this voyage was staged in the year 1919, A.D., in the state of Pennsylvania, United States of America, historians may someday find a parallel to the romantic tale of Vasco da Gama.

The main difference between the two voyages is that da Gama sailed the wide, wide sea, with Calcutta, India, his objective and conquest of land his ambition, while Captain Clark, in his 40-foot *Allegheny,* moved down the stream for which his boat was named under the propulsion of a four-horsepower engine—just to prove that the upper Allegheny River is navigable.

Then, da Gama set up a marble pillar at Calcutta as a mark of conquest and proof of his discovery; Captain Clark left it for the newspaper reporters who met him on the Pittsburgh wharf, at the completion of the voyage, to tell the world of his achievement. He left no other record for posterity.

Captain Clark believed that his achievement was being underrated by comparing it with that of da Gama. Da Gama's trip was like a modern voyage around Sandy Hook in a modern yacht, compared to his own, he declared. And he narrated the following story to prove this:

"We decided to build our boat. Here it is. The sleepless nights, pain and mental anguish, and other hardships we suffered were entirely unknown to da Gama and his courageous crew—but, of course, we felt, like all true discoverers, that real progress is born of suffering. We decided to build our boat at Olean, New York, but afterwards reconsidered and built her at West Hickory. We set sail—or rather, I mean, we cranked the engine on September 15th—and we have been on the way ever since, reaching Pittsburgh at 3 P.M., Saturday, October 18th, the same year.

"Our voyage was yet in infancy when our trials and troubles began. We were caught in shallow water and had to put out 'bat wings' to form false dams to let us out. At times we had to get out and push—yes, get right out in the water up to our waists—and push. Then again we had to hire a man—Craig Fry by name and 250 pounds in weight—to stand on the four-foot anchor to keep her down. Again we had to employ jacks to get our boat off the shoals, and on another occasion had to employ a team to get us out of the mud and off the rocks. Some nights when we could get ashore we slept in hotels. But there were nights when this was impossible and we had to sleep on the boat—on benches and the floor. One of the voyagers was sleeping on a bench back of the stove, when the boat turned on her side. The sleeper grabbed the hot stove pipe and got his hands blistered. We thought that was the end of our troubles, but last night we were caught in a heavy fog at Nadina, ten miles above Pittsburgh, and could not resume our voyage until daybreak, when the dense fog commenced to pass off.

"But we are here at last," concluded Captain Clark dramatically, and he jumped from the good ship *Allegheny* to the Pittsburgh wharf and lifted his hands in thankfulness as Columbus did on landing at San Salvador.

Captain Clark wanted the Allegheny to have some smoke pouring from her funnels like a regular steamboat as she passed the towns en route. Some mariners might have been nonplused by the fact that a small gas engine does not signify much smoke. But not Captain Clark. He simply set up a small cooking stove and burned scraps of tar paper in it, this creating enough smoke to blind curious people who stood on the bridges to watch the vessel go by.

This fantastic trip did create interest in the Allegheny River. Two large navigation dams have been completed since, extending year-round slack-water navigation high up as Brady's Bend, about 73 miles above Pittsburgh. Captain Tommy Clark died a few years ago. He would have died much richer, financially, if he had not spent money like water to direct attention to improvement of the Allegheny River.

The last time I saw Captain Tommy was the day the new Ninth Street bridge was dedicated at Pittsburgh. A county commissioner was making a long-winded speech, showing the pee-pul how he, single-handed, had caused the new bridge to be built higher above the surface of the river, so that steamboats could get under it the better. He alluded to his untiring efforts to forward the early improvement of the "noble stream" and he pointed to a brass plaque on which his name was displayed, in big lettering, perpetuating his memory forevermore— But the day was chilly and a cold wind whipped around the corners of adjacent buildings. I had heard enough, and turned to leave. There, pressed in the rear of the crowd, light overcoat pulled around his throat, unnoticed, stood Captain Tommy Clark. He got pneumonia soon after that, I think.

CHAPTER TWENTY-FOUR

THE surviving beauty spot of the Allegheny valley par excellence, lies south of Franklin, Pennsylvania. The river uses up 35 miles of its course going 15 miles to Emlenton. To accomplish this, it goes off on a leisurely excursion around broad bends, sometimes aiming for the Gulf of Mexico, oftentimes for the Atlantic seaboard, once or twice for Lake Superior, and for a mile or so very certainly toward the North Pole. While engaged upon this serpentine adventure, the river is buried deep in yawning mountain gorges. The section is inhabited by eagles and a few buzzards, mainly. The railroad which parallels the Allegheny most of the distance from Pittsburgh to Oil City takes one look at this primitive chaos and disappears through a tunnel for other fields to cinder. Once in a while an engine pops out of a hillside to survey the situation, only to pop promptly into another tunnel and scurry away again. High outcroppings of bare rock stand solitary sentinel on the hillsides and catch the direct rays of the afternoon sun and reflect them into the gloomy green vales below. At several points the sun comes up at 11:30 in the morning and sets at 1:30—so a native told us. This native was tending a "hillside" farm set at an angle of about 45 degrees. He placed his cabin at the foot of the farm; said it was a handy arrangement: on rainy days he need only look up the chimney and watch the corn grow above him. He planted the field by standing on the rooftop firing a shotgun loaded with corn kernels and with deadly aim. He didn't seem very reliable looking, otherwise, as I remember him: in my notebook, where these items were jotted, is a penciled (?) inasmuch as such hillside farming methods are pursued in Kentucky only, far as I know. One small town known as Kennerdale, drifted into this region by some mistake; the inhabitants have slowly become aware of the error and have been moving away, until now there isn't much left of it.

Geologists tell us that this section of the Allegheny is rather new. The original Allegheny River started at the headwaters of what now is the Clarion. The present Clarion valley was the upper Allegheny valley. The glaciers were responsible for the shift, and caused a river to slither down from Franklin and seek outlet into the Ohio-Mississippi system. As frequently attends such cataclysmic upheavals in nature, the result is splendid to look upon. The entire region is useless for farming, or lumbering, or railroad building, or highway construction, and with these patent advantages, has remained a beautiful cool paradise on a hot summer day, where silence screams to make itself heard, and vague scents of fragrant shrubs waft from glens and coves. A long-legged crane stands on a sandy bar at the head of a riffle watching for a fish and several wild ducks poke inquisitive bills among reeds in the shallow bars. There are no signs proclaiming this section as a "sanctuary" nor has it been turned into a park, or a reservation. A few fishermen have discovered access to the region and on a Sunday, or the Fourth of July, the "muskies" and the bass may ogle at wading boots casting rubbery brown and yellow gleams in the shoals, and notice peculiar artificial bugs switching along just below the surface.

On a high hillside at the southern end of this paradise, where the Clarion River empties into the Allegheny, stands an old stone mansion. Hidden in summer by oaks of tremendous girth, this homestead is barely visible from the channel of either stream. It is one of those queer places built by a man at the peak of his career; sort of "dream castle." The moment the place was ready for occupancy (as happens all too frequently) the builder up and died and left the whole outlandish adventure for his family to worry with. This is how the Fox homestead came into being. Joseph M. Fox, from Philadelphia, owned 118,000 acres in the early days and when he died his son, Joseph Mickle Fox, bought the Clarion property outright from the executors of the estate, worked hard, acquired money, and built the big house on top of the hill. Then he died.

The Fox homestead was built to last. Nearly a century old now, the stone walls stand as true as the day they were placed. I do not know what type of architecture was followed, but a description of it is fairly easy to present, and easy to understand: it is square and has a flat roof; there are two full floors and an attic with peekaboo windows. The cellar windows look like the third-floor windows except that they have square iron bars on them which would prevent anything larger than a house cat squeezing through. Aside from these iron bars and the ancient chimneys, the house could be stood upside down and nobody would appreciate the alteration until he looked for the front door. The building is monstrous (the rooms are high ceilinged) and it would serve conveniently as a hotel, or a post office, or a prison. It never has served as any of these things for the plain and simple reason that it is almost as inaccessible as Monticello. Today this building stands in lonesome grandeur there on top of the hill defying time. Remnants of huge shutters yaw wide open on broken hinges. A glimpse in one of the ancient windows discloses such an interior as a person might suspect, realizing that none of the family has lived there for years and years except for sporadic summer jaunts. An accumulation of "family furniture." Gloomy rooms full of treasures and junk, the house is ripe to go into business any day now as a full-fledged ghost factory.

When the builder of the Fox mansion died he left an only son, twenty-four years of age. This son married over east and came to the Clarion valley and occupied the big stone house and raised a family of two boys and two girls there and died just when the oil excitement started. His oldest son was William Logan Fox, a junior in the University of Pennsylvania when his dad died.

He went through Rensselaer Polytechnic at Troy and graduated four years later as a civil engineer, and went to Europe for about a year and finally gravitated to this Allegheny-Clarion homestead. William Logan Fox went to work and changed the whole countryside: there is scarce a square mile anywhere within thirty miles in any direction of the region which doesn't have some trace of this fellow's handiwork. Armed with a technical education, he built bridges, highways, buildings, and railroads. An enormous income from oil properties on and surrounding the Clarion lands provided a constantly refilled family treasury to pay the bills.

Foxburg, located a mile or so above the mouth of the Clarion River and on the east bank of the Allegheny, blossomed into the prettiest town along the stream. The Fox family put up a spacious school and a hotel, graded the streets, built houses, established a bank and nourished stores and other dwellings, and took care to keep the town free of the lawless element that was plentiful and abundant in the valley at the time. Transportation to Clarion, a fair-sized community up the river of that name, was at the mercy of poor roads and hacks; William Logan Fox built the Foxburg, St. Petersburg & Turkey City Railroad, a narrow-gauge triumph, which climbed hills that would balk a mountain goat and went around bends so sharp that the rear end of the train was in constant peril of collision with the locomotive out front. At Turkey City a connection was made with the Emlenton, Shippenville & Clarion Railroad. Eventually Mr. Fox consolidated the lines, ripped up the tracks to Emlenton, and expanded the Foxburg route so that it offered through service from Butler to Kane and points east. One day an official of the Baltimore & Ohio saw the railroad, fell in love with it (perhaps because of the zigzag feature) and bought it up. The narrow-gauge trains were replaced with standard rails and rolling stock.

In order to get this narrow-gauge into Clarion it was necessary to build numerous wooden trestles to span deep ravines, and one of these trestles, close to Clarion, was a miracle of the times, curved and single-tracked, over a dizzy and breath-taking hollow. One night a traveling salesman had imbibed somewhat freely and got in his rig and told the horse, "Home, Dobbin." Dobbin was used to the performance, but this time his master had managed to get drunk at a new location, somewhere near Clarion. The night was as black as the ace of spades but the horse, with true animal instinct, knew how to get home to the barn—at least he knew the general direction. Whether by accident or spurred by an urge of foolhardy enterprise, we do not know—only the horse knows—Dobbin left the road and drew the rig carrying the sound-asleep salesman out onto this frail wooden railroad trestle. The ties supporting the rails were centered one foot apart. The horse, undaunted, managed to get the wheels of the carriage fixed so those on the right side were outside the rails, and the left wheels were inside. (The muddy tracks told the whole story the next morning when a trackwalker discovered the evidence.) Dobbin, the sole witness of this miracle, managed to keep in the center of the tracks, and consistently stepped on the ties, and took the whole shebang clear across this chasm. Then he found the road again and when the salesman stirred himself and looked around, he was at the barn door and the old horse was waiting patiently to be let in.

This narrow-gauge railroad soon offered a story with a more dramatic twist. In February of 1880 a conductor threw a peddler off the passenger train near King's Mills for refusing to pay his fare. The peddler whipped out a gun and shot the conductor dead. The trial was to be held at Clarion, and William Logan Fox was to produce the pistol in court. He left home on the early train for Clarion and suddenly discovered he had forgotten to bring the pistol with him. The train was stopped and Fox ran back, got the evidence, and returned to the train in a very out-of-breath condition. He was twenty-nine years old and apparently well able to stand such strains, but nevertheless he collapsed and died within a short while.

The story does not end here. The peddler was convicted of second-degree murder and got eight years in the penitentiary. It seems he was a resident of St. Petersburg, a near-by hamlet, and was survived by a wife and a twelve-year-old son. Having no income, the son went to work for a farmer in the neighborhood and within a week, while crossing a field, a bull attacked him, ripped his side open, tossed him into the road. He died.

Foxburg's decline set in when William Logan Fox

expired in the narrow-gauge railroad coach. Projects for oil refineries, of additional railroad enterprises, and a general growth of the community were stilled. The Fox family erected a splendid church to his memory, and built a handsome library for the town: these are open for business today but, like many another project in the neighborhood, are not playing to capacity crowds.

There are many fine homes up the Allegheny valley built from oil money and lumber money. There are residential sections in Warren, and in Oil City, and in Franklin which are worth coming a long way to see —because once you catch sight of these places, from the exterior at least, you may grasp a vision on the "oil years." Matted by huge, expansive lawns, and framed by curious fences, these old homesteads are very much as you may imagine them to be; usually ostentatious, frilly, high-prowed, gewgawed, jimcracked, porched and pillared to a point of alarm. Forty or fifty years ago, the "fine and respectable" citizens lived in these jigsaw masterpieces. Today many of them have signs on the front walk-ways: TOURISTS ACCOMMODATED. A few have been turned into American Legion Posts, and Dorian Clubs, and the like. One thing I noticed, few of them are vacant. It is also true that the majority are painted and kept in good order. A sense of neatness, cleanliness, and orderliness pervades the entire Allegheny valley north of Franklin—this is a striking fact and true—if you shut your eyes passing Oil City.

CHAPTER TWENTY-FIVE

When eighteen-year-old William Logan Fox stood with bowed head and heard Scripture intoned at his father's grave in 1869, the huge stone house on the hill overlooking the Clarion and the Allegheny was filled with a buzz of suppressed excitement. Down over the fall of that hillside, past the big oak trees, lay a sleepy island at the confluence of the two rivers. There was a hum of activity down there. John Galey had drilled for oil on the island and a "hundred-barrel well" had come in. Immediately below, on the Allegheny's right shore, a small hamlet called Parkers Landing had stirred from a collection of a dozen hovels into a blooming city. The Fox domains, which stood for all that was decent and good, suddenly rubbed elbows with the most notorious sinkhole of iniquity, not excluding Pithole, which had sprung into being. The best and the worst of the valley were side by side!

Big wells were drilled in a new field over back of Parkers Landing. Hordes of men drifted in. Parker sprang in one jump from a crossroad nothingness to a city: the smallest city in the United States. In the short space of a year or so, the population jumped from a handful of local natives to a polyglot swarm of humanity numbering toward one thousand. One of the central features of the place was a large barge anchored at the wharf provided with women, wine and song, and over its sides was painted, in blazing letters: THE FLOATING PALACE.

The owner and master of ceremonies at the Floating Palace was one of the most notorious characters in the land. The mere mention of Ben Hogan was enough to cause chills along the spines of the God-fearing mortals of the neighborhood. Ben Hogan ran the Floating Palace. Ben's woman was "French Kate," and both had criminal records as long as your arm. Kate gravitated to the oil fields from Washington, D.C., where she had been in business of a dusky sort. She landed first at Pithole. There she set up a "variety show" which was reputed to be the only entertainment in the neighborhood which could make a hardened teamster blush. There she met Ben Hogan.

Ben had been a prize fighter on land, a pirate at sea, a bounty jumper and blockade runner, and prided himself on his title of the Wickedest Man in the World. After he had been sentenced to death for his crimes against the government, President Lincoln pardoned him and he landed in Pithole. He was "broke" when he arrived. Ben was of medium height, square shouldered, stout limbed, exceedingly muscular, and trained to use his fists. He taught sparring and gave exhibitions of strength at Diefenbach's variety hall. He fought Jack Holliday for a purse of six hundred dollars and defeated him in seven rounds in an arena packed with four hundred toughs, many of them armed to the teeth.

Ben's opponent at this fight was quite popular and the prediction had freely been handed around that if Ben walloped Jack Holliday he would be shot. After the final knockout blow in the seventh round, when Ben had been given the fight, there came a pistol crack and a z-z-zing! past Ben's head. A local champ named Marsh Elliott had fired the shot, but missed his target. As a queer afterclimax of this affair, Marsh Elliott got in the ring with Ben Hogan soon after and fought a four-round battle. He came out with a broken nose and a decisive defeat.

Hogan opened a palatial sporting house at Pithole after this celebration, and often took in high as a thousand dollars a day. He incurred the enmity of "Stonehouse Jack" and his desperado companions. A scheme was concocted in which a general brawl was to be staged in Hogan's emporium and Stonehouse Jack was to watch his opportunity and knock Hogan from the active list with a calculated bullet. Hogan learned of the plot, walked out to the street, saw Stonehouse Jack appearing from a dance hall. He opened fire on him, but his would-be assassin escaped to Titusville. The citizens of that city welcomed Jack with a huge celebration in which a gallows was erected on the main street. Then, led by an armed vigilante committee, Stonehouse Jack and his gang were escorted to a special train that took them out of the neighborhood.

When the Pithole bubble burst, and this wild West

movie thriller show was over, Ben and his "gal" French Kate started up operations on the Floating Palace at Parkers Landing. The Allegheny River protested against this abuse of its natural advantages and shoved the sin-palace up and down the bank, spewed ice gorges down upon it, and finally ousted this obnoxious mote from its anatomy.

Ben and Kate went over the hill to a new development called Petrolia and started up "Hogan's Castle." To follow their trail for the next four or five years is interesting diversion but the tale is principally loaded with crime and corruption and jumps all over the map. It winds up in New York City.

This book has a fence around it to keep it to the Allegheny valley but let us climb over it for a moment, since there is an excellent opportunity to present a Sunday-school moral on the other side of all this recitation of sordid doings. Ben Hogan dropped in to see a show on Broadway in New York in order to pass an hour or so, not suspecting the nature of the entertainment. Out on the stage walked Charles Sawyer, "the converted soak," and he opened a Bible. After reading some passages from the Scripture, Sawyer launched into a recitation of how he had been rescued from the gutter. Hogan fell like a ton of brick, signed the pledge at the conclusion of the service, went back to his hotel room and spent the night on his knees asking divine aid for the salvation of his person, which he suddenly realized was on the express route to perdition. The next morning he was in possession of a telegram from heaven or somewhere giving assurance that the angels would work on his case and he emerged with these words: "Peace fills my soul chock-full and I feel awfully happy."

Thereupon Hogan learned the alphabet so that he could read his way into becoming an evangelist. He showed French Kate the error of their routes, and there was a marriage ceremony. Kate did fairly well as a Christian for a time until she met some tough who struck her primitive fancy and she eloped with him. Hogan kept on, established his own sawdust trail, and met with varied receptions among audiences where he was well known in his more brilliantly sinful days. He kept it up for eighteen years. The Day of Judgment will hold special interest to those who knew him.

The city of Parker got along on its own momentum after the start Ben Hogan, French Kate, and the Floating Palace had given it. Presently two disastrous fires wiped out nine-tenths of the town, and very little was rebuilt, for by that time some gushers had been struck in the Bradford fields and the spotlight of activity had shifted northward.

Parker was not the only town scourged by fire during the oil days. Nearly every town along the Allegheny valley can look back to some specific date between 1869 and 1900 and locate a perilous conflagration. On June 5, 1892, there was a double-feature show when Titusville and Oil City had twin experiences such as are seldom chronicled in the affairs of mankind. Two milldams on the upper reaches of Oil Creek gave way during a sudden downpour and caused the failure of a

5,000 gallon tank of gasoline along the shore near Titusville. Creek water covered the streets and flooded out the gasworks and the electric plant. The city was in total darkness on that Sabbath night of early summer and, as frequently happens during a flood at that particular season of the year, the night air was damp and still; not a breath of wind was stirring. By midnight a visible mist, described as dense and white, lay over the creek forming a blanket a half mile long, a quarter mile wide, and several yards deep. What seemed to be a low-hanging fog turned out to be an explosive mixture of gasoline-mist. It is thought the open furnaces at the Cresent Works near by provided the spark. There came a terrific surge, a sheet of flame, and an explosion of first-rate proportions. Fifty lives were snuffed out and many homes burned.

Down at Oil City, at the mouth of the creek, a tank of benzine had been undermined by the rising water, had spilled, and this highly inflammable liquid had spread over the low-lying sections of the city. The Titusville horror was repeated. A wall of flame leaped high as the surrounding hills and a deafening roar shook the countryside.

CHAPTER TWENTY-SIX

IN THE tenth chapter of Joshua, twelfth verse, Joshua said this: "Sun, stand thou still upon Gibeon; and thou, Moon, in the valley of Ajalon." And the sun stood still for a whole day, and the moon stood still. The United States Engineer division of the War Department today is charged with accomplishing a similar feat, that of gentling the Allegheny River's disastrous floods.

One hundred and eight times in the past century Pittsburgh's "Golden Triangle," the downtown business district, has been inundated by rapid rises in the Allegheny. The flood stage at the mouth of the river is set at 25 feet. This means that when muddy water laps the gauge at that level, water pours over the tops of the banks, drowns out low-lying sections, halts some rail traffic, and makes a general nuisance of itself.

A common notion attributes river floods to the clearing of virgin forest lands which, in early times, blanketed the hillsides and meadowlands, and sopped up excess precipitation much as a dry sponge absorbs water, allowing it to drain off in leisurely fashion. The principal objection to this theory is the long-known fact that, prior to 1936, the greatest deluge occurred in March, 1763, when the river shot to 41.1 feet. This record stage was achieved before any of the timberland had been touched. In 1832, during February, the water got to 38.2 feet. In 1884, again in February, it went to 36.5 feet. In March of 1907, a stage of 38.7 feet was recorded. In 1913, a March flood crested at 33.6 feet. Pittsburgh settled down with a comfortable knowledge that the worst that could be expected would never exceed 40 feet. On March 18, 1936, the Allegheny slopped up to 46 feet, and the following year there was a repeat performance, with water lapping at the 35.1 foot mark.

By that time the United States Engineer Department had embarked on a scheme of flood protection. In order to accomplish this miracle, huge reservoir dams were projected for the major tributary streams of the Allegheny. The idea rapidly went into active construction work. Abnormal rainfall of the flood-producing variety will be caught and held in the upper tributary valleys, and released during dry seasons. The flood menace will be reduced. (Technical experts are cautious in their predictions and shy at the word "eliminate"—too much dead-end finality about it.)

Joshua's task was the larger, doubtless, for complex astronomical setups had to be tampered with; he well knew that his engineer corps could not handle the sun and moon problem—at least he did not seem to have sufficient faith in their ability to allow them to try a hand at the job. Joshua lived in Old Testament days

—but why go on about Joshua—we all know he was a righteous man and "in favor." When he found an adjustment of the planets (for certainly the sun didn't stand still; the earth and the moon froze their motions) desirable to the successful pursuit of his campaign, Joshua implored divine aid—and got it. A good bit of water has gone over the dam since those days, and now the United States Engineers must shift for themselves. Joshua's task was the larger, but the successful control of the Allegheny floods is the harder.

One of the principal reasons why flood control is a ticklish proposition is that the Allegheny River and its tributaries are spread over a huge area, an acreage so immense that abnormal rainfall may localize on one portion of the watershed and dump enough water into the streams to cause severe floods around Pittsburgh. Flood control dams, for this reason, are not positive flood protection unless great numbers of them are built, with the idea of having one waiting and ready at every point where a cloudburst might, by some remote or immediate possibility, occur. The subject is intricate, and a general statement of the problem is difficult, but that is the gist of it.

There is an organization in Pittsburgh called the Tri-State Authority, an outgrowth of an older group known as the Flood Control Commission. One or the other of these, along with newspapers, civic organizations, and the Allegheny River Improvement Association, has been hammering for flood reservoirs for quite a time—since the 1907 flood, I think—and still the job is unfinished. The total cost will exceed eighty-five million dollars, including similar treatment of the Monongahela River and its tributaries. Now then, when all these flood reservoirs are finished, and in operation, Pittsburgh's chances of having disastrous floods will be materially reduced. Every town and hamlet along the Allegheny and the Monongahela will also benefit. Fewer wet cellars; less hoisting of pianos onto stilts in living rooms and parlors. Even so, timid persons foresee the Sword of Damocles suspended over their heads.

An impounding reservoir once proved unreliable on a tributary of the Allegheny River. It let go during a period of abnormal rainfall and drowned so many people that the total is still in doubt, variously placed somewhere between 2,000 and 3,000 souls. Twelve million dollars' worth of houses, buildings, and barns went to Davy Jones in an hour or so. A wall of water came down a creek which, in ordinary times, was a mere trickle—not enough to float a steamboat—and slopped to a crest of 60 to 70 feet almost as quickly as you or I can climb a pair of stairs. There are seven hundred and seventy-nine graves in the cemetery at Johnstown, Pennsylvania, as a reminder of this deluge. A railroad bridge at the lower end of town caused a great part of the havoc, as its piers were closely placed, causing debris to jam upon them, and this wreckage, sopped with oil, caught fire: the whole mass was crawling with humanity. This happened in 1889, which seems a long time ago. The folks on the Allegheny were certain of two things for a long time after: (1) don't impound vast lakes of water above a city; (2) don't clutter up a river with piers of any sort. Today the passage of time has mellowed opinions, and the surviving lesson of the catastrophe just noted is in the form of a cardboard sign which you will see posted in shabby restaurants occasionally: "Don't spit on the floor; remember the Johnstown flood." These statements are presented with all sincerity.

So you see, all in all, the United States Engineers have a job on their hands. Joshua's accomplishment was quite positive in result, and didn't cost him one nickel. The harnessing of Allegheny River floods has a few "ifs" connected to it, and an expense account. Far more important than the flood protection element is the certainty that these new reservoir dams will be sound and substantial, and not swords held aloft by a human hair.

There is a tinge of irony in Pittsburgh's flood-control campaign. The expenditure of eighty-five million dollars will not protect the towns down the Ohio River below Pittsburgh. Oh, no. Just Pittsburgh and vicinity. If you have any doubts about this at all, it will pay you to take a trip down the Ohio River and look over the new flood walls which have been erected at every vulnerable city: Wellsville, Ohio; Huntington, West Virginia; Kenova, West Virginia; Portsmouth, Ohio; and so on down the line clear out to the Mississippi River at Cairo, Illinois. These walls are built to withstand floods such as swept down the valley in 1936 and 1937. Not a particle of interest was displayed in their design as regards the efficiency of the Allegheny River flood reservoir program. The practical-minded citizens of the Ohio River cities put up their walls just as though the Ohio River and all its tributaries was back in Indian days.

A great deal of money, public and otherwise, has been fooled away on river projects. The Allegheny is no exception. In the 1830's a canal was built up French Creek and connected Franklin, Pennsylvania, with Meadville. The ultimate object was the creation of a through waterway from Lake Erie to Pittsburgh. About a million and a quarter dollars were spent on a series of locks and a canal program. The total through traffic over this expensive waterway consisted of two canal-boats arriving in Meadville, on June 6 and November 14, 1834. There had been a "mistake" in calculating the volume of the stream at various seasons, and the project had no utility value.

No Congressional appropriations for Allegheny River improvement were authorized until 1878. Elsewhere in this book is a list of steamboats which have navigated the Allegheny. Virtually 90 per cent of them ran before 1878. The commerce on the stream had settled down to an old age of senility before one penny of public money was spent to better the channels. By that time the oil was going in pipe lines, railroads were hauling the freight, the iron and salt industries had disappeared from the valley for good and all. Lumber was coming down, and an extensive industry of barge building had sprung up; practically all the commerce was bound downstream. All the commerce that was left, that is.

The United States Engineer Department sized up the situation in 1878 and engaged upon a scheme of open-channel improvement, removing boulders, wrecks, debris, snags. And they built a series of low dikes to divert water to deeper channels. The entire program was designed to facilitate existing traffic. To the everlasting credit of the United States Engineers, the job was done thoroughly, thoughtfully, and permanently. A person cannot go over the history of the performance of this group of the United States Army service without gaining an admiration for the methods and policies of this Engineer Department. Ever since Colonel T. P. Roberts started wading around in Allegheny River water with a surveying instrument, every task that has been handed those engineers has been performed diligently and successfully. There is only one trouble with them: they are hard to get started on a job. Once they get started, it is doubly hard to get them stopped.

Navigation dams were built in the Allegheny River starting in with old Dam Number 1 at Pittsburgh in 1903. Since that date they have been extended up the stream until, in 1938, Dam Number 9 was completed, affording uninterrupted navigation for steamboat traffic a distance of some 70 miles to East Brady, Pennsylvania. At the present time there has been a positive halt on the construction of additional dams to carry navigation up to Franklin and Oil City. The United States Engineer Department takes the attitude that it "is from

Missouri" and wants proof that any further dams will pay for their keep in terms of traffic figures. They frown at the fact that no material tonnage developed after the last dam was built—no steamboats started chugging up to East Brady. This is true. Also it is true that the whole proposition is something like building a four-lane highway halfway from Miami to the Gulf of Mexico. If the builders stopped out in the middle of the Everglades and said, "Now, boys, show us some traffic or else she goes no farther," a person of average intelligence would suspect dirty work at the crossroads. To presuppose a volume of traffic on a half-completed highway which goes through a region of barren and forsaken wilderness is almost stupid. Yet, from present indications, no additional locks and dams will extend up the valley of the Allegheny until the United States Engineer Department sees some vigorous activity at the upper end of their completed project. How will the rivermen accomplish this? The answer to the riddle remains unsolved.

A small group of Pittsburgh rivermen made up their minds one day that the bridges spanning the Allegheny River in Pittsburgh's harbor were a menace to navigation. They trotted over to see Elihu Root, secretary of war, and asked for an order to get them hoisted to higher levels. An investigation resulted, in which Pittsburgh's newspapers had a lot of fun. The consensus of editorial opinion was that the campaign of improvement would cost somewhere near ten million dollars and the only resulting benefit would be that a score of flimsy little steamboats would run less chance getting their smokestacks knocked off in high-water times. Mr. Root smiled dismally and shook his head "no." This was in 1904.

Captain William B. Rodgers, a plucky, headstrong fellow who, by the way, was born in a houseboat at Franklin, up the Allegheny, was the ringleader in this program. The War Department's refusal to raise the bridges only served to whet his determination to get some action. Four years later, in 1908, he headed a delegation to the new secretary of war, William Howard Taft. Again the answer was negative. Captain Rodgers stuck his jaw out and went home. He was a veteran when it came to fighting. Many a Pittsburgher would elbow his way through a crowd to get a glimpse of this unusual warrior. In 1892, Captain Rodgers owned a small towboat named *Little Bill.* The Homestead mills of the Carnegie Steel Company were in the throes of a major labor strike and the recalcitrant workers had taken possession of the property. Henry Clay Frick engaged three hundred Pinkerton "watchmen" armed to the teeth and loaded them on a barge at Pittsburgh. Captain Rodgers volunteered to shove this impromptu army to Homestead with his *Little Bill.* There resulted a regular war, with many rounds of shot exchanged on both sides and Captain Rodgers up at the pilot wheel in the middle of the fray. The attempt to dislodge the strikers was unsuccessful, but the battle was a lively and prolonged one.

In 1911, the bridge-raising order was again refused by the secretary of war, J. M. Dickinson. Captain Rodgers and his small band of rivermen used every excuse for the next three or four years to further their aims. The large percentage of Pittsburgh's citizens did not take the matter seriously, feeling that Captain Rodgers was a little "hepped" on the subject and nobody in their sane senses would order such a program with so little benefit at stake.

Gradually the sentiment of the War Department commenced to change. Along came World War I and a renewed emphasis on the value of improved waterways. Secretary of War Newton D. Baker slipped into Pittsburgh on January 14, 1917, gave the offending bridges a "once-over," held a series of hearings, ordered them up. Pittsburgh newspapers broke out in scareheads, and columns of objections were printed. The order would be fought "to the last ditch" by civic authorities. This time the War Department meant business. The bridges went up in short order. A minimum clearance of 47 feet was observed in the alterations. Traffic, which had been dawdling around 2,000,000 tons annually, took a spurt and doubled itself by the time the changes were completed. Captain Rodgers and his associates were completely vindicated in their stand. Since that time the raised bridges have allowed various other improvements to be brought about to the benefit of Allegheny River navigation.

There are many rivermen who say that Captain Rodgers's death in the fall of 1925 was the greatest single setback to the immediate completion of the entire Allegheny River slack-water project.

CHAPTER TWENTY-SEVEN

THE modern Allegheny River valley is divided into three sections: like a bar of magnetic steel, there is surprising drawing power at either end and an absence of much activity in the center. The lower part, from Kittanning to Pittsburgh, is a beehive of modern industry, producing aluminum, plate glass, electricity, iron and steel, and so on. The extreme upper reaches, including Warren, Salamanca, and Olean, are alive and wriggling and full of "quick." Both these ends have a natural ability to draw new enterprise. The central portion of the river, between Tidioute and East Brady, is dead as a church on Monday morning by comparison.

Several generations ago the direct reverse was true: the lumber and oil exploitations reached zenith in the central section of the Allegheny valley and had things booming. Olean, the modern thriving New York city at the upper end of the stream, did not become a city until 1893. On the lower end, Aspinwall, Blawnox, Oakmont, New Kensington, Arnold, Brackenridge, and Ford City did not come into being until the heyday of lumber and oil was on the toboggan slide.

The impetus which caused Oil City, Franklin,

Tionesta, Tidioute, and other ports in the center of the valley to grow was clearly a "wildcat" circumstance. Times have changed and the world does not seem to yell for anything which Oil City and vicinity supplies these days. Perhaps this unfortunate circumstance may be due to a lack of advertising, I don't know; but I will try to be of some service: here are a few of the available assets I saw while up there recently.

For example, Oil City has a tempting supply of secondhand bricks, old sucker rods, empty oil tanks, a few choice smokestacks, and a wealth of oil-soaked real estate. There are two abandoned bridge piers at Franklin (badly in need of repair). Tionesta hasn't anything, not even a moving-picture show. There is a restaurant in Tidioute which harbors some fine stuffed fish; also a coon, I think. Some splendid dahlias are raised in the back yards at East Brady. I would mention the wonderful climate and the scenery, but obviously you can't haul that away in a tank car.

If this center portion of the valley is to recover someday, there is more than a strong suspicion that the rippling Allegheny River will have a whole lot to do with it. Oh, yes, the river today is neglected, abandoned, used as an open sewer and a trash basket. Yet it has the potentiality of a stick of dynamite.

Let us say, by way of illustration, that the United States Engineer Department concluded to extend the lock-and-dam system through the "ailing" portion of the Allegheny's anatomy. What would happen?

In order to get some idea of a correct answer, there is no need to speculate or guess. The Kanawha River in West Virginia is a striking parallel; also the Illinois. Both these streams have been improved; both have come ahead "full steam" since. The upper Mississippi is the latest example. What actually happens is the same as occurs when a four-lane boulevard is run through a crossroads town. Things you would not dream about take immediate root and commence to grow: new industries, establishments. Whole communities come into being where vacant real estate has gone begging since time immemorial. An improved river does these things on a more tremendous scale. No use to guess it would: put on your hat and go see.

It pays to treat a river right.

Up at Olean, the newspapers spell the river's name Allegany. Below the New York State line it becomes the Allegheny. Well, Allegany or Allegheny, she's a grand old river.

CHAPTER TWENTY-EIGHT

THERE is an old custom on rivers of the West, on which the Allegheny River is an important one, that a captain should say "good-bye" to his passengers when the end of the journey has come. This feeling is strong upon me now, for right here is where some books announce THE END and other books say FINIS, and still others (the great majority, I'm afraid) say nothing at all.

You have been a riverman for a time now, seeing the valleys, and the hills, and the towns—and the people, and the things people do—flow by the river. You have seen the shores flow and the mountains draw asunder.

Now you return to the normal state of being, and once again you see a river flow through a valley. How odd! for a time—or were we dreaming? The valley was flowing by the river. An illusion, perhaps. Yes, to most persons an illusion. To a steamboat pilot, and a raftsman, and a keelboater—the realest thing he knows.

ACKNOWLEDGMENTS

THERE were three books I never let out of my sight while this work was in preparation. The largest of these is called *The Allegheny River*. It was compiled by Serepta Kussart (Mrs. Phil Kussart), whose husband has been identified with dredging and contracting operations on the Allegheny for a good many years. These folks have a daughter Claire, and Claire has a modern Diesel towboat named for her which chugs a wicked stern wheel up and down the Allegheny's channels. Mrs. Kussart is chief historian for the Allegheny River Improvement Association, and had her history book published at her own expense a couple of years ago. The 342 pages of her work comprise a complete, accurate, and dependable account of each keelboat, flatboat, steamboat, and barge which has, for any reason, wandered into the Allegheny regions.

Sketches in Crude-Oil, the second source book on my list, was written by a kindly man from Oil City named John J. McLaurin. He lived up the Allegheny most of his life (perhaps all of it) and was a newspaper editor. His book, which came out in 1898, was published privately. He used to come to the meetings of the Allegheny River Boatmen's Association and was hailed with genuine joy by all who knew him. If my meddlings with his *Sketches* would have stained the pages of this book blue, and my gleanings of knowledge from Mrs. Kussart's *The Allegheny River* would have tinted things yellow, then this book would be a light-green tinge. Third, and perhaps most remarkable of all, is a small volume called *The Mammals of Pennsylvania and New Jersey,* printed in 1903 and authored by Samuel N. Rhoads. Strangely, this also was a privately published work. Mr. Rhoads went to extreme pains to gather firsthand information about the early wildlife of the Allegheny regions and presented an exhaustive study of the subject.

Dippings have been made into *Pittsburgh, The Story of a City,* by Leland D. Baldwin, University of Pittsburgh Press, 1937. Mr. Baldwin is without a doubt the best informed human being aboveground on the doings in early days of the Allegheny-Ohio basin. In 1917 the J. R. Weldin Company, Pittsburgh, brought out a reprint of *The History of Pittsburgh* by Neville B. Craig. This is a highly entertaining book of early times and tells some good stories. Seymour Dunbar's epic job, *A History of Travel in America,* also came into active use. Some of the material about the lead plates buried along the rivers came from Archer Butler Hulbert's *The Ohio River, Course of Empire.* The doings of Major George Washington were carefully followed through Washington Irving's *Life of George Washington* from an edition published in 1871. Mr. R. R. Jones, connected with the United States Engineer Department in Cincinnati published a map guide and reference book called *The Ohio River* in 1920, and this proved a valuable field of statistical information. Ethel C. Leahy, in 1931, brought out *Who's Who on the Ohio River,* which has much about the Allegheny River in it, being a fairly complete "What's What" as well as a "Who's Who." George H. Thurston's *Allegheny County's Hundred Years* has quite a deal of interesting and reliable steamboat information tucked away between its covers. *The Monongahela of Old*, privately printed by James Veech at Pittsburgh in 1892, contributed information. *History of Clarion County, Pa.*, by A. J. Davis, printed at Syracuse, New York, in 1887, is an important contributor to the general scene; as is *History of Venango County, Pa.*, by J. H. Newton, published at Columbus, Ohio, 1879. *A Few Scraps*, by Alfred Wilson Smiley, brought out by the Derrick Press, Oil City, Pennsylvania, is more than a few scraps, it is a good firsthand view of the oil days.

In a larger sense, the author is indebted to the *Waterways Journal*, a weekly trade paper devoted to the Mississippi and tributaries which hasn't missed an issue since it began business in 1887. Published at St. Louis, the files of this magazine are alive with firsthand, informally written accounts of the early days on the Allegheny River and elsewhere. The editor, Captain Donald T. Wright, is a native of Oil City and a chunk of his heart still is planted up around his native home which he deserted years ago to become one of the most widely known and popular boatmen on the Mississippi system. Recently a beacon light just below Lock Number 9, Allegheny River, was officially named "Donald T. Wright Light" in his honor and in recognition of the crusading he has done to improve river conditions. Special recognition is due editors of various daily newspapers, particularly George A. Zerr of the Pittsburgh *Post-Gazette*, who has been hammering out daily columns of "River News" for a quarter of a century with special attention to the Allegheny; and also George Stuart, editor of the Tarentum *Daily News*, who keeps his daily readers better informed on river topics than many a leading Cincinnati or Louisville metropolitan sheet.

A hearty thanks to Mrs. Adrian Rumbaugh, librarian of the Foxburg, Pennsylvania, Free Library, for capable assistance in locating material, and to unknown librarians in Pittsburgh, Olean—yes, even Wheeling, Cincinnati, and Louisville. Mr. Harold C. Putnam, an ardent river enthusiast at Warren, Pennsylvania, lent valuable aid, as also did Donald K. Slick of Oil City. A stream of letters to and from Edward S. Axline of New York City settled many an important point.

To one and all these persons, the author extends a heartfelt "Thank you."

STEAMBOATS

WHICH HAVE NAVIGATED THE ALLEGHENY

ADVANCE. A towboat of 39 tons which came out new in November, 1862. John and Benjamin Kunkel of Franklin, Pa., were interested in her along with Capt. David T. Lane. She did various Allegheny River work and also towed coal for the government during the Civil War along with the *Thistle, Hawk, Panther, Hornet,* and others. She was sold after one season to the Joseph P. Haigh Co. and one day blew up with the engineer out on the fantail.

ADVANCE NO. 2. This boat came out new in December, 1863, Capt. S. H. Marshall, master and part owner. Other stockholders came from Venango County, Pa. Under Capt. Bowser, in 1866, she ran packet trades on the Allegheny River, and in December, that year, she was sold to White River, Capt. James Dickey. I think Capt. David T. Lane of Franklin was one of her original stockholders also.

ALBION. A 50-ton packet built at Brownsville, Pa., about 1826 and ran that season in the Pittsburgh and Louisville trade on the Ohio River. In April, 1827, she went up the Allegheny to Kittanning, Capt. Pursall in command. She is credited as being the first steamboat to ascend the Allegheny that distance. Gen. William Robinson, Jr., of Allegheny, Pa., was a passenger. Upon arrival in Kittanning, the *Albion* took aboard an excursion party and went several miles above, returning the same day.

ALBION. A towboat. 130 x 21 x 3′ 10″. Drew two feet. Two boilers, 30 feet long, 40 inches diameter. Built in 1865 by William Munhall (for whom Munhall, Pa., is named) and Major William Frew and Charles Lockhart. Towed during the oil boom along with the *Brilliant* (which see) also owned by Capt. Munhall and others. Sunk by ice in the winter of 1875 and engines went to another towboat.

ALEX CHAMBERS. A towboat built in 1864. She had 2 boilers and 13's-4 ft.[1] machinery. Capt. George Estep was her master and part owner along with H. Estep, Alex Chambers, and John McNaught. Towed oil on the Allegheny.

ALEX FOSTER. Built at Pittsburgh in 1864, a towboat. Owned by Isreal Kiefer; sold later to Harvey Robinson. She had 2 boilers. Machinery 12's-4 ft. Towed oil on the Allegheny. Sank in the big ice, Monongahela River, winter of 1876.

ALEX HAYES. Mention of this towboat, but no facts available.

ALICE. A towboat with 13's-5 ft. engines operated by the Rodgers' Sand Co. of Pittsburgh. Built at Marietta, Ohio, 1892, as the *Charley Hook.* She towed sand and

[1] Rivermen visualize the relative power of various steamboats by quoting the cylinder dimensions: "thirteen's-four feet" means the *Alex Chambers,* in this instance, had cylinders of thirteen-inch bore and four feet stroke, or length. Quite a few river engineers on the Mississippi and tributaries can quote these mechanical dimensions for scores of boats, and keep them all straight, and seldom mix them up. No historical account of a western boat is satisfactory until the engine dimensions have been determined. The method of expressing these figures is just as presented, "thirteen's-four feet" or sometimes simply "thirteen's-four's."

gravel in the Allegheny River with frequency until she exploded her boilers August 30, 1913, on the Ohio River near Glenfield, Pa., killing eight of the crew and injuring two.

ALLEGHENY. Built at Pittsburgh 1818-19, owned by Adams, Wilson and Reno. 50 tons. As late as March 30, 1823, she was in operation in the Pittsburgh district and was a packet. On April 2, 1823, Capt. Reno in charge, she left for Arkansas River; apparently never returned.

ALLEGHENY. Stern-wheel packet, sometimes credited as being the first of that type built with the stern wheel exposed, the practice having been to enclose the wheel in a recess before her time. Launched at Pittsburgh, March 20, 1830, designed and owned by a Mr. Blanchard from Connecticut. She was the first steamboat to ascend the Allegheny River to Olean, N.Y. Left Pittsburgh, May 14, 1830, with 64 passengers and 25 tons of freight, and was in Warren on the 19th, on the 20th at Cornplanter, and on the 21st at 11 A.M. at Olean, N.Y. The boat had nine stockholders; three of them from Meadville, Pa. James and Lewis Follett were her pilots on this trip. Her dimensions were 91½ x 16′ 10″ x 2′ 7″. Some accounts say she had a double stern wheel. She had no figurehead, as was common practice in her day. The voyage to Olean was her third trip up the Allegheny, having previously journeyed to Oil Creek and to Kinzua. Sold to Cincinnati parties in 1831 and is known to have been running in the Pittsburgh and Cincinnati low-water trade late as 1835.

ALLEGHENY BELLE. This packet was built in 1842 at Elizabeth, Pa., on Monongahela River, Capt. John Hanna, master and owner. Machinery by Stackhouse & Nelson,

Pittsburgh. She came out in the Pittsburgh and Cincinnati trade during low-water season. Later when the water was up, she went in the Allegheny River packet trade between Pittsburgh and Franklin and stayed there eight years. Sank the *Ida* in collision at Tarentum on November 24, 1843, causing total loss of the *Ida* (which see). Capt. William Hanna was master in 1848. She was dismantled about 1850.

ALLEGHENY BELLE NO. 2. A packet owned by Capt. John and Capt. William Hanna, captained by the latter. Came out new in March, 1850, Pittsburgh and Franklin trade. On March 11, 1852, she "set the pace" between those two points on an upbound voyage. Her card:

To Freeport	3 hours 20 minutes
To Kittanning	5 hours 15 minutes
To Mahoning	6 hours 34 minutes
To Redbank	7 hours 45 minutes
To Catfish	8 hours 50 minutes
To Emlenton	11 hours 30 minutes
To Franklin	16 hours 30 minutes

She was retired about 1859.

ALLEGHENY BELLE NO. 3. A packet owned by these same Hanna brothers; came out new in December, 1850, and ran two trips a week to Franklin, Pa., and often up to Warren. She was contemporary with the *Allegheny Belle No. 2;* these were partner boats. Capt. C. W. Batchelor bought this boat in April, 1859, for the Louisiana Tehauntepec Co., for use on the Coatzacoalcos River and paid $9,000 for her. She was taken across the Gulf of Mexico and safely reached Minatitlán on May 18, 1859, with Capt. Andrew W. McKee in charge.

That fall Capt. McKee returned to Pittsburgh and built the *Lucy Gwin* for the Trinity River in Texas.

ALLEGHENY BELLE NO. 4. A packet which came out new in March, 1859, largely owned by Capt. John Hanna. Her master was Capt. William Hanna. Capt. John Hanna died at Oil City, Pa., on March 20, 1863, closing a long and active career as an Allegheny boatman, commencing in 1837 with the *Pulaski* (which see). His boats carried United States mail in the Pittsburgh and Franklin trade for many years. The *Allegheny Belle No. 4* was taken over by the government for Civil War purposes along with the *Leclaire* (which see) and went to Cincinnati, was found too small, and released, returning to the Allegheny River. After the death of Capt. John Hanna, this boat was sold to Commodore William J. Kountz and D. S. H. Gilmore for $21,000. Capt. George Moore came out skipper on her, and Dan Moore had a finger in the pie; she was placed in the Pittsburgh and Wheeling trade. Later sold to the lower Ohio and towed coal between Pomeroy and Cincinnati; this in 1863. Capt. John K. Booth had a boat of this name soon after—likely the same one.

ALLEGHENY CLIPPER. Hull built at Shousetown, Pa., in the summer of 1848. Owned by William C. Miller, John L. Abrams, Rees Rees, all of Pittsburgh, and Andrew Shaw of Jefferson County. Capt. William Watterson of Clarion County was her master. This was a 100-ton boat. She ran in the Pittsburgh and Cincinnati trade in low water, summer of 1849, during which time she came in collision with the *Ludlow*, a Pittsburgh and Zanesville packet; both were repaired. She ran to the upper Allegheny River when in her regular business.

John McClure, John Reed, and J. H. Roberts of Wheeling bought her in September, 1850, and took her away.

ALLEGHENY MAIL. A small packet, 77 tons, Capt. John Goff, master and part owner. Ran tramp trades, and came out new in August, 1844. A year later she was at Bradys Bend loading iron at the Great Western Iron Works for Cincinnati. Sold Feb. 9, 1846, to a Nashville, Tenn., concern for $5,000 to run from there to Smithland, Ky. Capt. Goff built the *Sunbeam* then for Ohio River trades.

AMARANTH. Built as a packet at Sharpsburg, Pa., in 1841. Side-wheel, 220 tons. Hull 147 x 25 x 5½. Two model barges also were built at the same time, 140 x 20 x 4, open hold with cargo boxes, for the upper Mississippi, 200 tons capacity each. Capt. G. W. Atcheson was her skipper. She was taken to the Mississippi while new and ran in the St. Louis and Galena trade. Sank at Amaranth Island, September, 1842. The name "Amaranth" means "unfading flower" used in a poetical sense. The name "stuck" in the upper Mississippi; three other packets bearing the same name being built from time to time—the last of the name sank on a snag at Smith's Bar above Doniphan, Mo., Nov. 17, 1867.

ANNIE LAVELLE. Towboat which came out new in December, 1865, owned by Swaney brothers of Venango County, and John Swaney was registered as master. She was caught by ice near Oil City in the later sixties. John J. Ormston, who owns a farm near by (1920), had many relics from this boat, including furniture from the cabin, flues, etc.

ANTELOPE. Built at Pittsburgh, a towboat, in 1865. Three boilers. 17's-6½ ft. stroke engines. M. F. Cassiday, R. G.

McKibben, and O. Edgar, owners. Master in 1867, Capt. James Y. Simpson. Brought oil out from upper Allegheny.

AQUILLA. Built at West Newton, Pa. A small packet of 59 tons. Came out new in August, 1854, owned by Capt. Jos. Nixon and Dan McAlier, of Pittsburgh. They built her for Monongahela River. In 1855 she ran passengers to Camp Meeting, two miles above Tarentum. Capt. Jos. Nixon was a prominent towboat man on the Ohio River—built a boat named for himself in 1877 which stayed in business until Dec. 12, 1938, somewhat of a record for a steamboat. The *Aquilla*, in 1856, went away—and up through the Fox River improvements which connect the Mississippi and Lake Michigan.

ARCHIE MASON. A 32-ton packet owned by Thomas, Edward, and Dennis A. Boland and commanded by Capt. J. W. Siddell, all of Allegheny, Pa. New in April, 1848. No other information available.

ARENA. Built by Capt. Joel C. Peebles at Elizabeth, Pa., and came out new in June, 1846. A small packet of 53 tons. Her first season was spent on the Monongahela. Capt. John Goff (see *Allegheny Mail*) went on her in the Allegheny River for several years. She withdrew in 1849.

ARROW. Small packet, 64 tons. Built in 1844 and was in Allegheny River trades through 1848. She was perhaps the first steamboat on the Allegheny River to sport a steam whistle. Capt. Andrew Miller was her first master. Capt. James Atkinson was on her in 1846, resigned in 1847 to go skipper of the *American Eagle* built for the upper Mississippi. Capt. William H. Gordon succeeded him. This boat ran on the Muskingum River at various times.

ARROWLINE. A 90-ton packet built for William B. Scaife in the summer of 1847. Came out in Allegheny River trades, Capt. Andrew J. Miller, that summer. Sold a year later to Lewis Martin of Bridgeport, Pa., for Monongahela River trades.

BEAVER NO. 2. A packet built in 1837 by T. S. Clarke, Robert Beer, and Capt. Jacob Poe, and commanded by Poe. She went into the Pittsburgh and Beaver trade connecting with canalboats. In 1838 she went into the Allegheny River, served as a packet, and made 14 round trips to Franklin, Pa., that season. Ran with the *New Castle* and *Pulaski* (which see). Dismantled in 1842 and her engines, etc., went into the *Bridgewater* (which see).

BELLE. A packet. Came out new at Pittsburgh in March, 1865, Capt. T. W. Laughrey. He and James Kennedy owned equal shares in her. A. Hartupee & Co. built the engines. Miller, Bunting & Co. of Pittsburgh put up the cabin. She was rated at 262 tons, the largest packet built for Allegheny River service. Drew 18 inches of water light. Hull was built at Monongahela City, Pa., by William Latta. Frank Whiting was her head clerk the first season. She left Pittsburgh on May 24, 1866, for Oil City, made the round trip and was back in 40 hours, fastest on record. This boat, under the command of Capt. T. W. Laughrey, in the winter of 1868-69, towed a circus in southern waters. In the spring of 1869 she was back in Pittsburgh, sold to J. V. McDonald & Co. for $9,000 to tow iron from Rochester to Portsmouth. Early in 1870 she was in the

Pittsburgh and Parkersburg trade, Capt. J. B. Smith; later operating as an independent packet on Monongahela River, same master. Early in 1871 she was sold to St. Louis and towed iron ore. There is a record of a packet named *Belle* in the triweekly New Orleans and Donaldsonville trade in 1878; same boat perhaps.

BLUE LODGE. A towboat with 17's-5 ft. engines built in 1866 and had three boilers. Owned by James Matthews. She was perhaps the largest towboat employed in the oil traffic on the Allegheny River and was soon withdrawn on account of her size. She went to United States marshal sale on January 6, 1874, at Pittsburgh and was sold to J. W. Williams for $13,500. The Grand Lake Coal Co. afterward had her; offered her for sale in 1876.

BOB CONNELL. Built in 1864 at Pittsburgh, a towboat. Had two boilers and engines 13's-4 ft. stroke. Owned by Alfred B. O'Neil and others. While towing oil on the Allegheny River her pilots were paid $25 a day and the steward got $200 a month. E. G. Gribble of Brownsville, Pa., bought her in October, 1900.

BRIDGEWATER. Built as a packet in 1843 and got parts from the old *Beaver No. 2* (which see). Capt. George W. Ebert was her master for a time. She also, during low-water times, ran in the Pittsburgh and Wheeling trade on the Ohio River, Capt. C. E. Clarke; her partner boat was the *Belmont*, Capt. Jacob Poe.

BRILLIANT. Towboat built at Pittsburgh in 1864. Capt. William Munhall, master and part owner. Three boilers, 16's-5½ ft. stroke engines. Companion boat to the *Albion* (which see). She ran in the oil trade on the Allegheny. Sold March 1, 1872, to Capt. Isaac Little,

Portsmouth, Ohio, and went to Ohio River towing. Blew up at Gallipolis, Ohio, later.

BUZZARD. A towboat employed in bringing metal down the Allegheny River in 1855. No details available.

CARBON. A towboat built at Elizabeth, Pa., in 1902. 117 x 23 x 4.5. Originally owned by the Monongahela River Consolidated Coal & Coke Co. Sold to the La Belle Iron Works of Steubenville, Ohio, in March, 1920. They opened a coal mine at Harmarville on the Allegheny, and this boat was engaged in "pooling" the barges to the Ohio River. Her master, Peter Hagan, fell overboard and was drowned in late October, 1919. This boat continues in operation in 1941, now owned by the Wheeling Steel Corporation.

CAR OF COMMERCE. Built at Freeport, Pa., in 1819 ior W. F. Peterson & Co., Louisville, Ky., from the *Rising States* (which see). This was a packet. Her name was perpetuated in various other packets of the same name on western rivers.

CHARLEY MCDONALD. A good-sized towboat built in 1871 and owned by Capt. J. V. McDonald (see *Convoy*). She had four boilers and 18's-7 ft. engines and towed out of Allegheny River. She was eventually sold south and towed around Pomeroy with Capt. H. M. Horton as master. Capt. Oscar F. Barrett bought her, and she was cut down by ice in the spring of 1899, and the wreck abandoned. Her whistle went on the Whiterock saltworks at Minersville, Ohio.

CHIEFTAIN. A towboat of 55 tons which came out new in September, 1847, Capt. John Campbell. Used on the Allegheny River.

CINDERELLA. A packet used on the Allegheny River in 1847. Hull dimensions 155 x 23 x 3. Two boilers, and engines 24's-4 ft. She was employed transferring passengers and freight from Freeport to Pittsburgh when the aqueduct for the Pennsylvania Canal burned that year. Capt. A. D. Reno was her master. After this job she went into the Pittsburgh and Wheeling trade and was commanded by Capt. George G. Calhoon, uncle of Capt. Thomas S. Calhoon of Georgetown, Pa. She was there in 1850.

CLARA FISHER. A packet built in the winter 1849–50 for Allegheny River, owned by Capt. William H. Gordon, G. E. Warner, and Amos Frisbee of Allegheny, Pa. She had two stockholders from Warren County also: Charles Fisher and E. G. Owens. Rated 108 tons. On March 22, 1852, she knocked her stacks down on a ferry cable at Sharpsburg and recovered $300 damages. In December, 1856, she hit a rock at Orchard Furnace, Allegheny River, loaded with flour and upbound. Returned to Pittsburgh for repairs. Was on the Allegheny in 1857 during the early spring months; she was sold then and went to Council Bluffs, Iowa.

CLARION. A packet built at Pittsburgh in 1841 of 42 tons. Capt. Alex Short was her master. Owned by Sidney Moreland and John B. Bell. Sold on November 10, 1841, to Muskingum River where she operated in 1842. Ben D. Richardson of Malta, Ohio, has a "waybill" issued from this boat's office in 1842.

CLARION. A packet built in the spring of 1851. Capt. Martin Millinger. Ran in the Pittsburgh and Zanesville trade during summer months and in the winter ran for a time in the Pittsburgh and West Newton trade on Youghiogheny River. Later operated in the Pittsburgh and Kittanning trade, three trips a week, often going high as Catfish.

CLYDE. A towboat owned by the Clyde Coal Co. of Pittsburgh which for years maintained a coal dock below the Sixth Street bridge. They sold her to Capt. Rush Burnside and she burned up near Pt. Pleasant, W.Va., about 1926.

COLLIER. Towboat built in spring of 1842, Capt. James Dalzell, master and owner. Ran on the Allegheny River.

CONVOY. A towboat of 123 tons built in 1854 for Allegheny River service and was owned by her captain, Erwin Creal, and John V. McDonald, both of Beaver County, Pa. She was running oil out of the Allegheny in 1861.

CORNPLANTER. A packet of 117 tons built at McKeesport, Pa. and came out new in April, 1851, owned by the Gordons, R. McCutcheon, John Miller, T. H. Reynolds, all of Pittsburgh, and M. Coleman of Kittanning. She ran up Allegheny River all that season, Capt. Wm. H. Gordon, master (see *Clara Fisher*). Capt. Gordon died during this season and Capt. Ezekiel Gordon replaced him. She was laid up for ice two miles below Bradys Bend on December 17, 1856, for ice; was cut down there during February, 1857, a total loss. Parts of the wreckage floated past Pittsburgh.

COTTAGE. A packet of 73 tons. Her hull was built at California, Pa., and she came out new in October, 1861. Cabin put up by Eichenbaum, Bunton & Co., Pittsburgh. She drew 12 inches light, was good for 150 tons of freight on 3-foot draft. Mary A. Saint owned half interest. Capt. John G. Saint was her master. J. J. Saint was the head clerk (brother of the captain). W. Russell was her pilot. She came in collision with the towboat *J. S. Cosgrave* (which see) above the Freeport aqueduct in early 1862 and 32 timbers in the hull of the *Cottage* were broken. A cabin was built on this boat in the summer of 1862 and she went to the Ohio River for low-water trades, and was sold that fall to Barker, Hart and Cook of Cincinnati.

COTTAGE NO. 2. A packet built at California, Pa., and came out new in November, 1862. Mary A. Saint owned half interest, same as in the original *Cottage*. Capt. J. G. Saint was skipper. As the Allegheny River was low, the maiden trip of this boat was to Cincinnati and back from Pittsburgh; then she entered Allegheny River packet trade. A cabin was placed on this boat in early spring of 1864 and she came out looking like a new boat. She ran several trips between Pittsburgh and Cincinnati and then was sold to Kanawha River. Her boilers exploded in December, 1865, and eight men were badly injured. She was rebuilt and used for some time after this accident. On March 21, 1869, she was towed up through the Pittsburgh harbor and was taken to Brownsville, Pa., and dismantled; her engines and equipment going to the *Mountain Belle* for Kanawha River. Capt. W. F. Gregory was the pilot on watch when the *Cottage No. 2* exploded and Charles Finney was his partner. Capt. Newton was master. Luther Vance was clerk. Len Faulkner and William Curtis were the engineers, Faulkner was on watch. Capt. Ralph Hamilton was one of the passengers aboard, en route to Malden, W.Va., to see a sick sister.

CREIGHTON. A towboat on Allegheny River owned by the Pittsburgh Plate Glass Co. She was sold to Kanawha

River and dismantled down there; her boilers went to the *James Sutherland;* this about 1939.

DANIEL BUSHNELL. Towboat built at Pittsburgh in 1856. Capt. James Matthews was her master in 1866, when she was engaged towing oil well supplies on the Allegheny River. She had two boilers, and 14's-4 ft. engines.

DIAMOND. A towboat employed in sand and gravel towing on the Allegheny River, which exploded her boilers at Bellevue, Pa., about 1913. She was originally the towboat *S. B. Goucher* and her machinery, originally from the *Vigilant,* later went on the *Iron City* of the Iron City Sand Co.

DICK FULTON. A towboat built at Elizabeth, Pa., in 1857. Capt. Phillip R. Hill, owner and master. This boat was on the Allegheny River in the fall of 1861, towing oil. (See *Hawkeye* for further news of Captain Hill.)

DICK FULTON NO. 2. A towboat which came out new at Pittsburgh in 1860. She towed oil on the Allegheny in 1861, owned by Thomas and George Jones, B. F. Wilson, and Capt. W. Cunningham, her master. This boat came in collision with the *Hawkeye* at the "Point," Pittsburgh, Feb. 5, 1864, and Alex Martin, her engineer, was drowned. Of interest may be the fact that two other steamboats named *Dick Fulton* ran on the Ohio River in later years.

D. T. LANE. A towboat with three boilers and 16's-5½ foot stroke engines built in 1871 by David Torondo Lane (see *Advance*). Lane bought the old side-wheel packet *Ingomar* from Reuben M. Thomas, Steve Thompson, Fred Kimple, and others, which was in the Pittsburgh and Matamoras trade in the sixties. The *Ingomar* had engines from a Civil War side-wheeler called *General*

Thomas. Parts of these engines were built into the towboat *D. T. Lane,* which was constructed on the banks of the Allegheny River. Lane also used the engine-room bells, capstan, and other items which had seen service on the *General Thomas*. This towboat *D. T. Lane* was a bigger financial job than Lane anticipated, and Capt. W. Harry Brown advanced funds for her completion, and eventually took her over, and ran her for a time. David Lane went to Franklin, Pa., and set up a machine shop there. The Campbells Creek Coal Co. on Kanawha River bought the *D. T. Lane,* used her many years, rebuilt her frequently, and she did service until she was dismantled at Reed, W.Va. in October, 1937.

ECHO. A packet of 100 tons which came out new in March, 1858. Alexander Campbell of Bradys Bend was principal owner. Capt. Ezekiel Gordon (see *Cornplanter*) was master. John Conner and Henry Bollinger were the pilots. She got to Franklin on her first trip on April 4, 1858. When the oil boom struck the country this boat was one of the four regular packets then in operation, the others being the *Allegheny Belle No. 4, Venango, Leclaire* (which see). In the fall of 1862, Ben Coursin was sole owner of this boat and Capt. Gordon was still her master. She was sold December 26, 1862, to Sunfish, Ohio, parties for the Pittsburgh and Gallipolis trade. Capt. James Walton took principal interest in her and Josephus Walton the balance, both of Monroe County, Ohio.

ECHO NO. 2. A packet on the Allegheny which came out new in June, 1863, owned by Capt. Thomas M. Rees and Capt. Ezekiel Gordon. Her hull was built at California, Pa. The government bought this boat in the fall of 1863 for $20,000.

ECHO NO. 3. A packet which came out new in January, 1864, principally owned by Capt. James H. Rees of Pittsburgh and the remainder by Ben Coursin of McKeesport, Pa. She was rated at 147 tons. Capt. Ezekiel Gordon was her master. She went into the Pittsburgh and Oil City trade, Jan. 30, 1864.

ECLIPSE. A small boat, Capt. R. T. White, operating on the lower Allegheny in 1851.

EGLANTINE. A small boat of 25 tons which came out new in December, 1861. Owned and mastered by Capt. William Lloyd of Allegheny, Pa. In the summer of 1862, Capt. Josiah King was on her. That fall J. T. Deffenbacker bought her—she ran in the Allegheny River.

ELIZABETH. A packet of 52 tons, owned and commanded by Capt. J. J. Davis, Pittsburgh. Ran in the Pittsburgh and Franklin trade in the season of 1839, along with the *Forest, Beaver, Pulaski* (which see). She was still there in 1841, partly owned by John Goff; she was rebuilt that summer and renamed *Kittanning* (which see).

ELIZABETH SMITH. Built at Point Pleasant, W.Va., in the winter of 1916-17 for J. K. Davison & Bros., sand and gravel operators. Capt. Wm. L. Cavett was her master. She measured 127 x 23 x 4. Machinery 14's-6 ft. and had three boilers. This boat replaced the *Lee H. Brooks* (which see). Her machinery came from a ferry called the *City of Cairo*. On March 25, 1936, she sank near Jack's Island, Allegheny River, was raised, Capt. Wm. Cavett still in command. Today, 1941, she still remains in active business, popularly known as the "Lizzy."

ELLA LAYMAN. A towboat new at Pittsburgh in fall of 1872. Rated at 119 tons, owned by Edgar Layman. She went to Oil City, Pa., in the spring of 1877 and got a tow of "greasedom products" for delivery at Huntington, W.Va., under command of Capt. Jack Parrish. Considerable interest was evidenced at Oil City inasmuch as she was the first boat to tow oil from that place in two years. She worked principally for the Standard Oil Co.

ENTERPRISE. A towboat built on the river bank at Allegheny, Pa., in 1833, owned in part and captained by David Blackstock.

EXQUISITE. A towboat built up Allegheny River in 1879 and was probably the first tunnel-stern propeller boat on western rivers. Capt. Ephriam Ralph built her. He sold this boat to B. S. White of Shreveport, La., in 1882 to tow cotton.

FLORENCE BELLE. Built in 1892, hull at the Axton yard in Brownsville, Pa., and machinery from Jas. Rees & Sons Co., Pittsburgh. This packet was 150 x 27 x 3. Had engines 13's-4 ft. Owned by Capt. H. Page Hudson of Freeport, Pa., and Capt. T. P. Hudson of Clinton, Pa. The former had a daughter named Florence and the latter a daughter named Belle. This boat came out in April, 1895, Capt. H. P. Hudson, master. Ran with the *Nellie Hudson No. 3* on the Allegheny River in the Pittsburgh, East Brady and Catfish trade, making occasional trips to Oil City, Pa. Made her last visit to Oil City in May, 1897, and was the last steam packet to visit that town. She was transferred to the Pittsburgh and Morgantown trade on the Monongahela River in the summer of 1897. Cut down by ice at Creighton, Pa., in January, 1910.

FORD CITY. A small towboat operated on the Allegheny by Krantz and McCoy. She burned March 27, 1915, at Ninth Street, Pittsburgh, along with the *Oriole*.

FOREST. A packet on the Allegheny River built at Pittsburgh in 1839, owned and captained by Capt. William Ward, a farm boy from up Chartiers Creek, who got on the river and variously owned and ran the *New Castle, Forest, Orphan Boy, Warren,* later made a fortune in real estate. This packet *Forest* collided with the *Pulaski* while downbound from Warren, Pa., at a point about 20 miles above Pittsburgh on the night of May 5, 1843 and sank the latter; this being the first serious accident on the Allegheny.

FORT PITT. Built at Brownsville, Pa., and came out new in October, 1848, Capt. A. D. Miller, owner and master. She was a packet of 130 tons. Ran on the Allegheny River until early 1850 when sold into the Pittsburgh and Nashville trade.

FRANK FOWLER. A small towboat on the Allegheny River in recent years, owned by the Pittsburgh Plate Glass Co. towing between Creighton and Ford City in 1918. She went through several changes of ownership, finally burned.

FRANKLIN. A packet of 33 tons, new at Pittsburgh in September, 1844, Capt. Hugh Dennison, master (see *Ida* and *Wilmington*). Her maiden trip was to Cincinnati and return with 12 inches on the Pittsburgh marks. She was regularly in the Allegheny River that winter.

In 1845 Capt. James Wilkins was her master and the owners were David Grier and J. A. Stockton of Pittsburgh. She got new boilers in the spring of 1845 and later branched out to operate on the Ohio River in the Pittsburgh and Beaver trade and then went to the Monongahela River, Capt. Abrams. In low-water times she was also employed on the Muskingum.

FRED HUDSON. A towboat built at Hickory, Pa., up the Allegheny River in 1910 and was the last steamboat built up that stream. 124.2 x 26 x 5. She operated around Pittsburgh and in the Allegheny until sold to Capt. Ralph Emerson in December, 1917. In February, 1918, she left Pittsburgh with a large barge loaded with knocked-down steel freight cars consigned to New Orleans which had been loaded at the McKees Rocks plant of the Pressed Steel Car Co. Capt. Graham Varble was master. She was sold again to a Vicksburg concern in January, 1920.

FREEDOM. A towboat of 33 tons owned by Hugh and Andrew G. Smith. Came out new in April, 1847, and ran on the Allegheny several years, Capt. Jos. Stephens.

GENERAL LARIMER. A towboat built in 1854 at Elizabeth, Pa., and in 1861 was towing oil on the Allegheny River, owned by Capt. William Abrams of Rimerton, Pa. She was a large boat, had three boilers, 15's-4 ft. engines. In 1870 she was still in operation, owned by James Jackson, Sr. and commanded by Robert Jackson.

GEORGE THOMPSON. A towboat on Allegheny River in 1860. In May that year her master, Capt. John Thompson, was drowned near Sixth Street bridge, Pittsburgh. In 1861 this boat was owned by Capt. Joseph Walton, and he was aboard her as captain and the towboat was employed taking coal and empty oil barrels up the Allegheny. In 1862 she was owned by Hamilton McLintock and her master was Capt. Uriah Walton.

GIPSEY. A towboat built at Pittsburgh in 1864. Capt. David Brenneman was her master in 1867. She had three boilers and engines were 15's-5 ft. stroke. Used on the Allegheny River.

GIPSEY NO. 2. Came out new in November, 1865, Capt. W. H. Laughlin, owner and master, along with other Beaver County, Pa., parties. Towed on the Allegheny. The engines from this boat, or else the original *Gipsey*, later went on the towboat *I. N. Bunton*.

GREENBACK. A towboat built in 1865 and had two boilers and engines 10's-3½ ft. stroke. Capt. John Rodgers was her master in 1867. She was sold to the government along with the *Tidioute* (which see) and became a United States survey boat, towing derrickboats, removing snags, etc.

GREENWOOD. A 47-ton passenger boat which ran between Pittsburgh and Manchester (suburb) carrying people to and from Greenwood Gardens, owned by James McKain. Came out in April, 1848. Was sold that fall to Kentucky River.

GREY FOX. A towboat which came out new at Pittsburgh in October, 1857. Rated 70 tons. In 1862 she was owned by Capt. J. V. McDonald and others. George Vandergrift, engineer of this boat, drowned in late March, 1862, when he fell overboard a short distance below Oil City, Pa. His body was recovered near Sewickley, Pa., on the Ohio River. This boat saw much service in the oil- and coal-towing business on the Allegheny.

HARRY NO. 2. A small towboat owned by the Pittsburgh Plate Glass Co. in 1918. Seems to me she exploded herself in the end.

HAWKEYE. Built at West Newton, Pa., by Capt. T. W. Fowler and came out about 1854, a towboat. In 1861 she was engaged in the oil trade on the Allegheny, then owned by Jacob Hill.

HAWKEYE NO. 2. Built at Pittsburgh in 1863. Three boilers, and engines 16's-6 ft. stroke. She came in collision with the *Dick Fulton No. 2* (which see) at the "Point" in Pittsburgh, Feb. 5, 1864. In 1865 she was owned in equal shares by S. J. Carr and Walter Tetley. Engaged in oil towing on the Allegheny.

HERCULES. Small towboat on the Allegheny in 1854.

HERO. A towboat owned by James Scott and commanded by him, built 1867 at Pittsburgh. Two boilers, and engines 11's-4 ft. Towed on the Allegheny.

HEROINE. Mention, towboat of oil days. No record available.

H. H. DENNIS. A small boat of 38 tons built at Pittsburgh in October, 1861. Capt. Alfred Wilcox was her master and part owner. Other stockholders were A. C. Williams and Charles G. Brown of New York State. She left Pittsburgh October 29, 1861, for the upper Allegheny. Engines 12's-3½ ft. stroke. One locomotive boiler.

HOPE. A towboat built in 1842, Capt. Daniel Bushnell, owner. Capt. William Lapsley, master. Towed coal from the Bushnell mine, near the present Glenwood bridge, Monongahela River, to points on the Allegheny.

HOPE NO. 2. A 50-ton towboat owned by John and James Matthews and commanded by the latter. Came out new in February, 1848, at Pittsburgh. Used on the Allegheny.

HUNTER. Small towboat on the Allegheny in 1854.

HYENA. Towboat built at Pittsburgh, 1864. Engines 14's-5 ft. Two boilers. Owned 1868 by Joseph Keeling. Capt. John Grime, master. Towed oil on the Allegheny.

IDA. An Allegheny River packet built in 1842, Capt. Hugh Dennison. Sank a total loss in collision with the *Allegheny Belle* (which see) near Tarentum, Pa., on Nov. 24, 1843. She was replaced with the *Wilmington* (which see) in 1844.

IDA REES. This was an Allegheny River packet, and she came out new in November, 1863, built at a cost of $15,000. Rated at 221 tons. Owned by Capt. Thomas M. Rees and Capt. James H. Rees of Pittsburgh. Her master was Capt. Ezekiel Gordon. Her first exploit was a trip from Pittsburgh to Nashville, Tenn., and return. Capt. Rees Rees later commanded her in the Allegheny River. Wintered at Oil City, 1863-64, and got shoved out on the bank by ice and had to be moved in. In November, 1865, she made a special trip from Pittsburgh to St. Louis with 2,700 barrels of oil for W. P. Logan of Pittsburgh. Capt. Joseph Brown later used her in Ohio River trades. In the spring of 1868 she made a trip up the Missouri River in charge of Capt. James Rees. On Nov. 11, 1868, she left Pittsburgh and went to New Orleans, Galveston, and Trinity River in Texas, Capt. Thomas Stubblefield in charge. She sank Feb. 28, 1873, in the Sabine River en route to New Orleans with a cargo of 500 bales of cotton.

IDA REES NO. 2. This 284-ton packet came out new in December, 1865, owned by Capt. Thomas M. Rees and Capt. James H. Rees. Her master was Capt. Rees Rees. She entered the Pittsburgh and Oil City trade. Henry

C. Frye and Jacob Magee were her pilots. Thomas Mariner was mate. She was the biggest and best Allegheny packet of her day. This boat and the original *Ida Rees* ran as partner boats in 1866. Came down from Oil City, arriving in Pittsburgh on May 24, 1868, and quit the trade—the last trip made by a boat of the Allegheny River Navigation Co. and last of the Oil City packets. During the summer of 1868 she ran in the Pittsburgh, Brownsville, and Geneva trade on the Monongahela River. She was sold at public auction at Pittsburgh on Sept. 1, 1868, for $3,800 to Capt. James Rees. Made a round trip to Memphis, Capt. G. W. Albert, master, and James H. Rees, clerk. In the spring of 1869 she was lengthened 20 feet, and left Pittsburgh on April 1, 1869, Capt. Thompson, master, and went to the Missouri River. On this voyage she ran clear up to Fort Benton, Mont., and had a famed race with the *Importer* and beat her, often related in Missouri steamboat lore. She sank in June, 1871, with a big cargo aboard. Her owners on the Missouri River were Durfee & Peck, and Capt. John Gillam was her master. She was snagged near White River, 23 miles below Chamberlain, S. D. Her cargo consisted of valuable furs and robes, reported worth $100,000. The loss of the boat was placed at $20,000.

IMPERIAL. A towboat of 222 tons which came out new in October, 1865, at Pittsburgh and made trips up the Allegheny. Capt. W. Peddler, master and owner.

IRON CITY. Towboat of 41 tons. Came out in November, 1846, owned and mastered by Capt. J. Marlatt, of Allegheny, Pa. Ran principally on the Allegheny River.

IRON CITY. A towboat, new in August, 1873, owned by E. A. Elsey, George W. McCrackin, and W. R. Riddle.

Her master was Capt. Warren Elsey. In April, 1877, this boat stranded at Pithole, Pa., and remained there all summer, a crib dam made of crossties was made to keep her afloat. She was released by a rising river in October, that year. She ended her career by grounding on a gas main at Herrs Island, Allegheny River, and in attempting to work off, the main was broken, and the escaping gas took fire from her furnace and she burned, a total loss.

IRON CITY. A towboat owned by the Iron City Sand Co. and built at Parkersburg, W.Va., about 1912. She burned in August, 1934, was rebuilt. Still in service, 1941.

ISAAC WALTON. A 9-ton boat, intended as a pleasure craft, came out new in September, 1841, owned by R. W. Lindsay and Henry A. Emmons, but during low water that season was engaged as a commercial vessel.

JACOB PAINTER. Towboat built at Pittsburgh in 1859. Two boilers, and engines 14's-5 ft. stroke. Originally owned by Abraham Hays; later by Tom Fawcett, S. Packer, and others. Used on the Allegheny.

JACOB PAINTER NO. 2. Towboat owned by Abraham Hays, and was new at Pittsburgh in 1865. Used on the Allegheny.

JAMES JACKSON. Towboat built by Robert Jackson and others at Pittsburgh in 1871. She had three boilers and engines 13's-5 ft. stroke. She long towed Allegheny River oil to Parkersburg and Huntington; so used for about ten years. She sank at Sewickley, Pa., on Oct. 31, 1878; ran into an old coal barge during a storm. Was raised. She belonged to the Citizens Oil Refining Co. at the time of this accident. James Jackson, Esq., for whom the boat was named, died at Wilkinsburg, Pa., in July, 1921, aged eighty-three.

J. D. James. A packet built at Warren, Pa., in the spring of 1860 to ply between there and Tidioute, Pa.

Jenny Lind. A packet built at Zanesville, Ohio, and came out new in the Zanesville and Beverly trade, being unable to get out of the Muskingum River by reason of a broken dam which blocked navigation at the time, this being in 1848. In 1850 she was in Allegheny River trades taking the place of the *Reveille*. She was again in the Allegheny in 1859 after the *Allegheny Belle No. 4* had been sold south. There is some possibility that this 1859 boat was a second *Jenny Lind*, as records show the original boat of that name having been sold to a circus outfit named Spaulding, Rodgers & Van Orden at Rockport, Ind., in October, 1851, to take the place of the *Loyalhanna* which had just sunk.

Jim Watson. Towboat of 60 tons which came out new at Pittsburgh owned by Capt. Thomas M. Rees. Capt. L. F. L. Vandergrift was her first commander. Sold to Adam Becker in 1862 and Capt. Charlie Bears was on her; during which period she was in service towing oil on the Allegheny River. Twice sold in 1863 and finally bought by Valentine Horton of Mason City, W.Va.

John F. Dravo. Towboat which came out in 1867, rated at 148 tons. Owned by L. P. and F. Chester, the latter acting as master. She had 16½'s-4½ ft. stroke engines. Used on the Allegheny River.

John Hanna. Towboat built at Pittsburgh in 1865. Daniel Dempsey and William Hanna were her owners. She was a good-sized boat, had three boilers, and engines 16's-5½ ft. stroke. Commanded by Capt. Daniel Dempsey. She was named to honor Capt. John Hanna who ran the fleet of *Allegheny Belle* (which see) packets; also the *Pulaski* (which see) and others. This boat was rated at 236 tons and had a long career on the Allegheny River towing oil and supplies. She was sold to Pomeroy, Ohio, parties in April, 1879, and towed on the lower Ohio and Kanawha rivers. Capt. John C. Cooper was a third owner in her during this time. The boat was finally dismantled and her engines went to the Bay Line packet *Henry M. Stanley*.

J. P. THORN. A Pittsburgh towboat new in summer of 1878, owned by George J. Free, William Ross, and others. Rated at 120 tons. Her first trip was from the Allegheny River to Huntington, W.Va., with seven barges of oil consigned to the C. & O. railroad for delivery to Richmond, Va.

J. S. COSGRAVE. Towboat built at Pittsburgh in 1858. Two boilers and engines 13's-5 ft. stroke. Owned by John Munhall and others of McKeesport, Pa. Towed oil on the Allegheny after 1860. In early 1862 she rammed the packet *Cottage* (which see) damaging the latter. In 1863 she was owned by the Pennsylvania Salt Mfg. Co. In 1868 she was owned by Willis Hodgson and captained by him.

JUNIATA. Built in 1841, a towboat. John Schoenberger, owner, of Pittsburgh. Rated at 21 tons. Dismantled in 1847. Capt. Joseph Stephenson was her master.

JUNIATA NO. 2. Built in 1847 and replaced former towboat of the same name. Also owned by John Schoenberger.

JUNIATA NO. 3. Came out new September, 1852, owned by George and J. H. Schoenberger. Her master was Capt. A. Brauff. This was a 30-ton towboat.

JUSTICE. A 75-ton packet which came out new in the fall of 1851, Capt. Joseph Skelton, master. She was on the Allegheny River in 1852. She was built at West Newton, Pa., and owned by John and F. Steiner and others of that place. Came in collision with the *Clarion* about 14 miles above Pittsburgh and the *Justice* got her paddle wheel knocked off. After repairs she ran in the Pittsburgh and Sunfish trade that summer. At the close of the spring season, 1853, she was withdrawn from the Allegheny River and sold to St. Louis parties in July, 1854, for $6,500 and went to the St. Louis and Dubuque trade.

KANGAROO. Towboat built at Pittsburgh in 1865 and owned by David Clark and others. Capt. John A. Hughes was her master. She had two boilers and engines 12's-4 ft. stroke. Used on the Allegheny. In December, 1878, she went to Cincinnati with five barges of Allegheny River cobblestones for paving purposes.

KEYSTONE. Towboat built in 1865 at Pittsburgh and owned by Thomas Renouf and others. She had three boilers and 16's-5½ ft. engines. Used in oil trade on the Allegheny River.

KITTANNING. A packet new in 1841, having previously been the packet *Elizabeth* (which see), but was rebuilt and lengthened. Capt. John Hanna was her master the first year. Capt. John Goff was her skipper in 1842. This boat ran Allegheny River trades.

KITTANNING. Towboat belonging to the United States Engineer Department, Pittsburgh district. Built in the spring of 1916 at Lock Four boatyard, Monongahela River, and came to Pittsburgh on her maiden trip on March 30, 1916, with Capt. Silas Sayre in charge. Most notable achievement of this boat was a trip to Oil City, Pa., and return in 1928, arranged by Col. Jarvis J. Bain and Capt. Donald T. Wright. She reached Oil City at 6:30 P.M. on March 31, 1928, being the first steamboat arrival there in many years. There was a stage of 7 feet on the gauge at Oil City when the boat got there. The voyage was made to demonstrate the practical aspects of navigation to that point and much popular interest was evidenced. Several years later the *Kittanning* sank a total loss at Dashields Dam, Ohio River, engaged in towing at that place.

LA BELLE. Modern steel towboat of the Wheeling Steel Corp. built in 1920 at Jeffersonville, Ind., and still engaged in Allegheny River, towing coal out from Harmarville. She has compound 15's-28's-7 ft. stroke engines.

LAURA NO. 2. This towboat came out new at Pittsburgh in December, 1864, owned by Capt. R. B. Bell of Venango County, Pa., and ran on the Allegheny River. She was rated at 60 tons.

LAWRENCE. Built at Lawrenceville, a suburb of Pittsburgh, in spring of 1845, owned by Capt. Jeremiah Lawrence and Samuel Copeland. This was a small boat of 9 tons, plied the Allegheny River.

L. C. MCCORMICK. A packet built in spring of 1872 and owned by William McCormick and J. M. Phillips of Pittsburgh. Ran excursions on the Allegheny River and did packet work, and was sold on June 7, 1875, to James Martin and Charles Buck and taken to the Muskingum River. This James Martin later built the *Gen.*

H. F. Devol and others on the Muskingum, and he was master of the *L. C. McCormick* there, and the clerks were N. Kincaide and C. A. Buck. Her pilot was Capt. William Richardson. On Feb. 16, 1879, she exploded her boilers on the Muskingum River and was a total loss. Some years later a farmer in the vicinity was plowing a field, came across a shaving mug which had been blown from the boat, identified it as belonging to Capt. Richardson, and returned it to its owner; today Capt. Richardson's son keeps that mug as a prized relic.

LECLAIRE. This was a packet of 93 tons built for Allegheny River service, coming out new in November, 1859. Capt. John Ross was her master and part owner, along with Hamilton Kelly, both of Kittanning. She cost $8,000 when built. During the summer of 1863 she ran in the Pittsburgh and Parkersburg trade on the Ohio River, but was back up the Allegheny that fall. In November, that year, she knocked a hole in her bottom at Catfish Riffle and was out of service awhile for repairs. In the spring of 1864 she was in the Wheeling and Parkersburg trade and in April was sold to Capt. Samuel Christy, Wm. T. Thayer, T. J. Bottsford, for Kanawha River service.

LECLAIRE NO. 2. A packet which came out new in October, 1864, at Pittsburgh, Capt. Hamilton Kelly of Kittanning the sole owner. She ran in Allegheny River trades until February, 1867, when she was bought by Capt. J. G. Saint and reoutfitted and taken to the Missouri River where she made several trips to the "mountains." Later she again changed owners and ran in the Louisville and Tennessee River trades; sank at Brandenburg,

Ky., on Dec. 15, 1867, but was raised. Another time she sank on the falls at Louisville but was raised. Still again she struck a field of ice on the upper Mississippi and sank, this below Davenport. Again raised. She was sold July 23, 1870, at Louisville to T. Ballard for $9,000. Two years later she was again sold to the E. H. & N. railroad for $7,000. Finally sank at Evansville and Capt. Robert Hornbrook wrecked her as she was a menace to traffic at his public wharfboat. While owned by Ballard, she was in the Louisville and Evansville trade; Capt. A. Ballard was her master, and P. B. Branham and L. H. Branham were her clerks.

LEE H. BROOKS. Built in 1890 at Evansville, Ind., as a short-trade packet, 140.5 x 23 x 3.4, and named for the president of the Coney Island Co. of Cincinnati. She ran in short trades out of Cincinnati and in 1896 had a female mate—a rare event—Mrs. Helen M. Young of Ironton, Ohio. Later this boat was converted into a towboat and went to the Allegheny River to tow for the J. K. Davison & Bros. sand and gravel interests and Capt. Tom Hudson was her master. When the *Elizabeth Smith* (which see) was built, the *Brooks* was sold to Capt. W. L. Berry of Paducah, Ky.

LIBERTY. A small towboat of 24 tons which came out new at Pittsburgh in May, 1847 owned by Nicholas Whitfield. Capt. F. W. Fowler was her master. Capt. Dan Fry one time told the author that this boat was later owned by Capt. Jake Hill and commanded by his son, Capt. P. R. Hill. This was the first boat, according to Capt. Fry, which towed iron ore in guipers from Pittsburgh to the Allegheny River furnaces—the ore coming from Lake Superior regions after the railroads were opened. There is record that the *Liberty* overturned at Dam No. 1, Monongahela River, in December, 1848. In passing, it may be of interest to record that these guipers were decked flats about 125 to 135 feet in length and 16 feet wide with oak bottoms and pine rakes. There were numerous iron furnaces between Pittsburgh and Franklin which were supplied with ore by river.

LIBERTY NO. 2. This towboat was new in 1852, Capt. Thomas W. Fowler, owner and master. This boat and the *Buzzard* (which see) towed metal down the Allegheny in 1855 and on June 19, that year, she struck a pier of the St. Clair Street bridge, Pittsburgh, and sank a total loss.

LIBERTY NO. 3. A towboat of 54 tons, new in the fall of 1860, owned by William and John Pedder and commanded by Capt. William Pedder. In 1861 she was engaged in towing oil-well supplies up the Allegheny and bringing oil out. This boat was eventually sold to Capt. John K. Booth and saw service on the Ohio River, and when dismantled the *Liberty No. 4* was built, a famed towboat which operated between Parkersburg and Cincinnati on the Ohio River for the B. & O. Railroad, before the B. & O. S. W. was completed. This latter boat was also owned and run by Capt. John K. Booth.

LITTLE JIM REES. A towboat built by Capt. James Rees and James McGovern in 1864, and the latter was her master. She had two boilers, and engines 13's-5½ ft. stroke. On April 5, 1869, she was sold to the Grand Tower Coal Co. of St. Louis for $8,500 and left the Allegheny regions.

LOUISVILLE. A towboat built in 1864 and had two boilers and engines 14's-5 ft. stroke. Capt. Robert M. Boles was her first master on the Allegheny River, towing oil and supplies. She was sold in 1869 to R. J. Wheeler of Stillwater, Minn., for $7,000. She was taken to the upper Mississippi River and had a long and bright career towing rafts of lumber.

MAJOR ADRIAN. A small packet built to operate between Pittsburgh and Meadville, Pa., and came out new in July, 1852, Capt. David Edgar master. She ran until September, 1853, and then was sold to Capt. Sam Humbertson and David Fletcher of Ogle County, Illinois.

MARY ANN. A packet built at Elizabeth, Pa., and came out new in the fall of 1846 for Allegheny River service, owned by David A. Grier. Capt. Hugh Dennison was her master. Her engines were built by Rowe & Davis, Pittsburgh, and the cabin (she had 32 staterooms) was put up by Owens and Ross, Pittsburgh. During the low water of 1848 this boat, commanded by Capt. Robert Duncan, went to Missouri River on an extensive trip. On the return voyage she sank near Marietta on a snag; was raised. Snags those days were called "Polk stalks" because President Polk wouldn't supply funds to have them removed from the rivers. She re-entered the Allegheny River packet trade in December, 1848, making two round trips a week to Franklin. On Jan. 16, 1849, she was struck by two coalboats which had torn loose from their moorings, sank. She was torn down, a new hull built, engines, etc., transferred over, and she came out again for Ohio River service owned by Capt. Alex McGowan and R. E. McGowan.

MARY DAVAGE. A 3-boiler towboat built in 1865 at Pittsburgh with 16's-5½ ft. stroke engines; used on the Allegheny at times. Capt. James Clegg was master and part owner. In 1868 Capt. James Sheddin was her master. Was still in operation, 1869.

M. D. WAYMAN. A towboat built at Tarentum, Pa., in 1891 by the Pittsburgh Plate Glass Co., 146.5 x 27.5, and had 15's-5 ft. stroke engines. Capt. Harry Hulings got her in 1907 and operated her until 1918; then sold her to the Carnegie Steel Co. for an astonishing price—something like $50,000.

MONITOR. A small towboat built by James Rees at Pittsburgh in 1862 and used on the Allegheny. Later sold to the Armstrongs at Wheeling. Burned at Bellaire, Ohio, Oct. 14, 1885.

MONTEREY. Built in 1862 and was a towboat. Had two boilers and 11's-4 ft. engines; used on the Allegheny.

MOTIVE. A towboat operating on the Allegheny River in 1847, making trips to Franklin Furnace for pig iron.

NATRONA. A towboat new in November, 1863, owned by the Pennsylvania Salt Mfg. Co. and commanded by Capt. William Russell. Rated at 111 tons. She grounded crossways at Charleys Oven, below Franklin in March, 1864, and things looked critical for a while, but she got away. The Allegheny Valley Railroad bought her in early 1867 and converted her into a packet, connecting with their line then under construction. In May, 1868, she came to Pittsburgh from Red Bank, having been sold, and loaded out with freight and emigrants and departed for the upper Missouri River.

NEBRASKA. A low-water packet built at Kittanning, Pa., in the fall of 1853 and owned by J. K. Wright of that place. She had a patent boiler and one cylinder. Cog-wheels, flywheels, belts, and other fixings. Ran on the Allegheny.

NELLIE HUDSON. A stern-wheel packet built in the summer of 1886 at Clinton, Pa., for the Hudson family. She was 141.3 x 25 x 3.4. Got her engines from the *W. R. Jones,* and entered the Pittsburgh and Kittanning trade, Capt. John S. Hudson master. During the fall of 1886 she made a low-water inspection trip down the Ohio River and then entered the Pittsburgh and Parkersburg trade, as the Allegheny was low and she could not operate there. Made her initial voyage in the Pittsburgh and Kittanning trade, leaving Pittsburgh on March 22, 1887; first packet up the Allegheny in eighteen years. The venture was fairly successful. She was sold to Capt. Lewis Vandergrift of New Harmony, Ind., and went to Wabash River. About a year after that she was again sold to Capt. S. H. Parisot of Vicksburg and was used on the Yazoo and Sunflower; late in 1890 she sank at Vicksburg.

NELLIE HUDSON NO. 2. Built for Capt. H. P. Hudson on the bank of the Allegheny River above Freeport, Pa., and was 158 x 28.6 x 3.4. Had engines 12's-5 ft. stroke, and two boilers. Sported a calliope. Ran in the Pittsburgh and East Brady trade and in low-water seasons did business on the Monongahela in the Pittsburgh and Elizabeth trade and ferried to the Pittsburgh Exposition. Sold through Capt. C. W. Batchelor to Indian River in Florida in 1892, and her name was changed at Pittsburgh to *Santa Lucia.* Capt. Fred W. Swerger of Brentwood, Pa., took her down; she was 50 days en route from New Orleans to Indian River. Henry M.

Flagler was her purchaser. The date of the construction of the *Nellie Hudson No. 2* was 1889.

NELLIE HUDSON NO. 3. Hull was built at Brownsville, Pa., and she was brought down to Pittsburgh on March 31, 1893, and engines and boilers were installed by James Rees & Sons Co. On May 30, 1893, she made her trial trip on the Allegheny; Capt. John S. Hudson of Kittanning was enrolled as master. She was 141 x 25 x 4. She ran on the Allegheny until 1897 when she and the *Florence Belle* (which see) were transferred to the Monongahela River. Later she made various trips up the Allegheny to bring down new barges, etc., and eventually was cut down by ice at Ford City, Pa., in 1913.

NEW CASTLE. In steamboat history, but two steamboats ever went to Olean, N.Y., on the Allegheny River; first being the *Allegheny* (which see) and last being this little packet *New Castle*. She was built at Freedom, Pa., by Stephen Phillips & Co. for the Pittsburgh and Beaver trade to connect with canalboats, and operated along with the *Fallston*. Both were stern-wheel and small —the *New Castle* was about 40 tons. Her hull dimensions: 100 x 16½ x 3½. Had a single 2-flue boiler and engines of 11½-inch diameter. She was sold to a number of Allegheny River merchants in 1837 and under the command of Capt. Josh Leach went to Olean that year. In 1838, on May 18, she went up the Kiskiminetas River as far as Leechburg, Pa., and is the only steamboat on record to achieve such a trip.

OIL CITY. Came out new on June 1, 1863, a packet of 59 tons, owned by George W. Morton, Wm. Anderson, Dan O'Neil, and O. King. Capt. John Noss was her master. She ran up the Allegheny that spring; was sold to Wheeling parties late that fall. Sank at North Wheeling on March 30, 1865, but was apparently repaired, as there is record of her existence on Muskingum River in 1868 with Capt. D. Lyne as master and Jas. Patterson as clerk.

OIL EXCHANGE. A packet, new in November, 1863, built for Allegheny service, owned by Capt. John Steiner of Venango County, Pennsylvania.

OIL VALLEY. A towboat owned by the Jackson family, and Capt. Thomas Jackson was master. Built in 1865 and had three boilers, and engines 15's-5 ft. stroke. She is recorded as the first boat to take a tow of oil products from Pittsburgh to New Orleans, Capt. James Jackson in command. In the spring of 1870 she was back on the Allegheny and on April 4, that year, she struck a pier of the Emlenton bridge, a total loss; a colored cook and his son were drowned. The boilers and engines were later salvaged and placed on the *Oil Valley No. 2* (which see).

OIL VALLEY NO. 2. A towboat built at Pittsburgh in 1870 and got engines and boilers from the original *Oil Valley*. Owned by Thomas Jackson and William Jackson. She took the first tow of benzine to Memphis from the Allegheny River and also towed to St. Louis. She was sold to Sam Casle in early 1872 and again sold to the McDonalds in the same year, and sank while they had her, but was raised. In 1873 she was sold to Henderson, Ky., parties and did service as a transfer boat between there and Evansville. Later the Campbells Creek Coal Co. on Kanawha River bought her for coal-towing purposes and she made frequent trips through to New

Orleans. Capt. John F. Rust made his first trip south on her after getting his pilot's license in 1878. Capt. James Summers of Gallipolis was then in command. Her name was changed to *Spring Hill,* and she was wrecked at Lock Five, Kanawha River. The wreckage was raised, and the engines, etc. went over to a new boat called the *R. K. Wells* which eventually burned near Charleston, W.Va.

ONEOTA. Hull built at Elizabeth, Pa., for Capt. William Ward (see *Forest, Orphan Boy*) and she was completed at Pittsburgh in August, 1846. This boat replaced the *Warren* (which see) and ran trips to Warren, Pa. She was about 37 tons.

ORIOLE. A small towboat used on the Allegheny River which burned on March 27, 1915, along with the *Ford City* (which see) at Ninth Street, Pittsburgh.

ORPHAN BOY. A small packet built for Capt. William Ward (see *Forest*) and ran in Allegheny River during 1841.

PANTHER. A towboat built at Pittsburgh in 1863 for Jos. P. Haigh, and her first captain was C. H. Cochran. She had four boilers and engines 20's-7 ft. stroke. On April 7, 1864, she rammed a barge loaded with metal into a pier of the P.R.R. bridge at Pittsburgh and sank it. Towed iron out of the Allegheny for several years and was sold later to H. D. Hutson. Still in operation, 1867.

PARK PAINTER. A towboat built in 1868 by Capt. James H. Rees, J. C. McLaughlin, and Thomas Cavett. She had two boilers and engines were 12's-4½ ft. stroke. Ran on the Allegheny with Capt. Thomas Cavett as master. This venerable captain had six sons: John, Howard, and Pres were engineers; Thomas Lee, Bill, and

Ed were pilots and captains. They owned and ran the *Cora, Clara Cavett, Park Painter, Uncle Sam, Park Painter No. 2.*

PARK PAINTER NO. 2. Towboat built in 1871 and had two boilers and engines were 13's-5 ft. stroke. She saw most of her active existence on the Allegheny River.

PATHFINDER. Towboat in 1842 on the Allegheny. Her engineer, Norman Gleason, fell overboard and was drowned near the mouth of Deer Creek in August that year.

PAULINE. An Allegheny River packet in 1839 owned by Samuel Hartman of Pittsburgh. Rated at 53 tons. Capt. John Tucker was her master. She was sold to William Ward (see *Forest*) and John Speer about 1840.

PEERLESS. A packet new in October, 1865, built for Allegheny River service, Capt. A. D. Russell in command. She was rated at 275 tons; made her maiden trip to Oil City leaving Pittsburgh on Oct. 23, 1865, with Albert Hancock as clerk. Soon went to the Ohio River and was converted into a towboat.

PETROLIA. A packet built at Pittsburgh and came out new in May, 1864. Rated 100 tons. Hamilton McClintock owned most of the stock. Capt. W. H. Kinter was her commander for the first month, then was succeeded by Capt. John Gordon. She ran up the Allegheny, and on Nov. 18, 1864, going under the Freeport aqueduct, she knocked off her pilothouse leaving pilot and pilotwheel intact. On December 20, 1864, while leaving Parkers Landing, a steering oar from a near-by raft came into a stateroom, badly injured the occupant. This boat wound up in the Black and White Rivers of the south, carrying United States mail. She sank in 1871, a total loss.

PETROLIA NO. 2. Built by the same owners of the original boat of this name, and the *Petrolia No. 2* was contemporary, coming out in July, 1864, a new boat under the command of Capt. Uriah Walton. Hamilton McClintock, who owned most of her, was a Venango County oil man. She made an unusual trip from Pittsburgh to Oil City and return in August, 1864, on a "pop" rise in the river. The Allegheny Valley Railroad bought her in the early spring of 1866 to make connections while their roadbed was being constructed between Mahoning and Bradys Bend. Later she was sold to the lower Ohio and entered the Evansville, Owensboro, and Cannelton trade, and was there in November, 1869, with Capt. John H. Triplett as master and John A. Adams as clerk. She eventually returned to Pittsburgh and sank at the wharf there on Jan. 3, 1873, was raised and converted into a towboat.

PILOT NO. 2. A packet, regularly engaged on the Ohio River, but pressed to Allegheny River service between Freeport and Pittsburgh in 1847 when the aqueduct burned, interrupting service of the Pennsylvania Canal. She was owned by Capt. William J. Kountz, who also had the *Yankee* (which see) there.

PITTSBURGH & WHEELING PACKET. Built in 1827 by Phillips and Graham of Phillipsburg, Pa., near the mouth of the Beaver River. In February, 1828, she made a trip to Kittanning and was the second boat to ascend the Allegheny River that distance. First was the *Albion* (which see).

PRAIRIE BIRD. A packet of 83 tons, and she came out new at Pittsburgh in June, 1845, owned by Capt. John Vandergrift who was a son of Capt. Jacob Vandergrift, well-known figure on western rivers. Capt. Jacob's wife was a cousin of Captain Jacob Strader and Capt. Jesse Hart, prominent steamboat operators on the lower Ohio and the Mississippi. The *Prairie Bird* went into the Pittsburgh and Cincinnati trade and her pilots were William J. Kountz and C. W. Batchelor; it was on the second trip in this trade that Batchelor met Eliza Vandergrift, who later became his wife. Later Capt. Vandergrift sold this boat to Wheeling parties and, under the command of Capt. Mellor, she went to Warren, Pa., in June, 1847, and brought down 1,395 barrels of flour for Forsyth & Co., Pittsburgh.

PULASKI. A packet built at Pittsburgh in 1837, with Dr. Robert Wray of Pittsburgh as owner and Capt. James Varner as master. She ran that season down the Ohio River and was up the Cumberland River far as Nashville. That fall she went in the Allegheny River trade, arrived at Franklin on November 26th and went to Tionesta. Capt. John Hanna was her master. In 1838 she made fourteen trips to Franklin and occasionally went above to Brokenstraw Creek, which is just below Warren. In 1839 she was still in that trade. On the night of May 5, 1843, the *Forest,* downbound from Warren, struck this boat about 20 miles above Pittsburgh, sank her. Steampipes let go, scalding many persons—first serious accident on the Allegheny River. She was raised and towed to Pittsburgh by the *Allegheny Belle* (1st). Burned at the Pittsburgh wharf on March 3, 1844, in a fire of suspicious origin.

RARITAN. A packet built at Sharpsburg, Pa., in 1840 and ran down the Ohio River, Capt. Alex Short.

RED FOX. Towboat built at Brownsville, Pa., in 1854 by Capt. J. J. Vandergrift and others. Rated 78 tons. Towed oil out of the Allegheny in 1861 and later was sold to the government on the lower rivers. Sank at Cairo, Ill.

REVEILLE. A packet of 71 tons built at Pittsburgh and came out in the fall of 1849 owned by William Colvin, Alexander Goff, and Robert Major, all of Pittsburgh. Capt. H. M. Stone was her master. She ran in Ohio River trades. Later Capt. Rees Rees went skipper and she made trips up the Allegheny. On occasion she was withdrawn and the Muskingum packet *Jenny Lind* was chartered to take her place. The *Reveille* was sold on Oct. 10, 1850, to Ezekiel Day of Pittsburgh and J. H. Gallagher of McKeesport. Later she was in the Pittsburgh and Wellsville trade down the Ohio River, Capt. Shedd; then was sold to Capt. Brubaker for the Pomeroy and Portsmouth trade.

RISING STATES. A packet of 150 tons built at Freeport, Pa., and was the first steamboat built at that place. This was in the winter of 1818-19. She came out new in March, 1919. J. Whiting & Co. of Pittsburgh were her builders and W. F. Peterson & Co. of Louisville, Ky., her owners. Her name was later changed to *Car of Commerce* (which see).

ROBERT SEMPLE. Built at Pittsburgh in 1871 for Capt. Thomas M. Rees, and her master was Capt. I. N. H. Carter. Had three boilers and engines 13's-5 ft. Ran on the Allegheny River.

Samuel Snowden. A packet which came out new in March, 1853, and made irregular trips up the Allegheny River that season. Capt. W. P. Torrence was master.

Science. A packet which came out new at Pittsburgh in March, 1860, and was regularly an Ohio River steamer. Capt. William Reno was her master and also half owner, the balance of her held by S. C. Young and others. On Feb. 5, 1861, this boat loaded up with empty oil barrels for Franklin. She was forced to turn back about halfway and brought a cargo of salt out with her. Later she made many trips up the Allegheny River.

Sharpsburg Packet. The name was longer than the boat, apparently. She ran in local trades on the Allegheny in 1850.

Skipper. A small packet commanded by Capt. William Stoops which saw service on the Allegheny River in 1847 running between Pittsburgh and Freeport when the aqueduct burned and service on the Pennsylvania Canal was stopped. Soon as this job was over the *Skipper* skipped into the Pittsburgh and Sunfish trade, Capt. Stoops, and later ran on the Muskingum.

Star. A boat of 54 tons, new at Pittsburgh in March, 1848, owned by John Whigam, A. B. Gallatin, and James O'Neil. Capt. Robert McClure of McKeesport, Pa., was her master. On May 27, 1848, Capt. McClure fell asleep in a chair, tipped overboard, was drowned; this was four miles below Freeport, Pa., and the boat was upbound at the time. Further the deponent knoweth not.

Tempest. Built at Pittsburgh in the spring of 1849, owned by J. W. Samuel and Wm. H. Clark. Took the place of the *Thomas Scott* in the Greenwood Gardens trade.

THOMAS SCOTT. A small boat of 50 tons built in the spring of 1849 and owned in part by James Irwin of Elizabeth, Pa., and Capt. Jos. Vandergrift and B. B. and George Vandergrift of Pittsburgh. She ran in the excursion trade to Greenwood Gardens (Manchester, North Side, Pittsburgh) and was speedy—could go down in 7 minutes and return in 10 minutes. Was in the Pittsburgh and Kittanning trade in December, 1850. On the 18th of that month she collided with the Sharpsburg ferry and knocked the ferry pilot into the river. She was withdrawn from this trade in early 1852.

THREE LIGHTS. A towboat built in 1869 and had two boilers and engines 14's-4 ft. stroke. Originally owned by James Mathews. Sold at a United States marshal sale on Jan. 6, 1874, to Capt. William Barnes for $15,000. All this while the boat had been employed in the oil traffic on the Allegheny River. She was caught in the big ice of 1877 and wrecked. Possibly she was repaired, for there is evidence of her being in the possession of Capt. W. H. Moore in 1879, and it is said she was renamed *Wm. Kraft*.

TIBER. A towboat new in March, 1862, owned by Capt. John Rodgers and others, styling themselves as R. D. Cochran & Co. She was rated at 92 tons. In six weeks during the spring of 1862 this boat brought 10,000 barrels of oil down the Allegheny and took 6,000 empty barrels upstream to the oil fields.

TIDE. A towboat built in 1881 at Clarington, Ohio. Hull was 117 x 22 x 3.6. Owned by Capt. William B. Rodgers, Sr. and frequently towed on the Allegheny River. About 1900 she was taken into the Monongahela River Consolidated Coal & Coke Co., Pittsburgh, and cared for the "flat" trade, delivering fuel to mills on the Allegheny. Capt. Billy England was long her master. Later she was sold to the Diamond Coal & Coke Co., Pittsburgh; then to the Reliable Towing Co. and finally to the National Transportation Co. and burned at Grays Landing, 81 miles up the Monongahela River from Pittsburgh, in late October, 1924, along with the *Robert Jenkins.*

TIDIOUTE. A small boat of 63 tons new at Pittsburgh in the fall of 1863 owned and mastered by Capt. Amasa Dingley of Warren County, Pennsylvania. She had engines from the lakes, brought from Erie, Pa., and ran on 8 inches of water. After some Allegheny River operation she was sold to the government and her name was changed to *Major Sanders,* to honor the gentleman of that name who then was topographical engineer in charge of the Ohio River.

TRAVELER. Built in 1839 by James, George, William, and Anthony Fawcett. Capt. Jim Fawcett was master. Ran on the Allegheny River.

TRAVELER. A towboat built at Pittsburgh in 1864 by William and John Pedder and Earnest Succop. She had two boilers and engines 13's-5 ft. stroke. She saw service in the oil trade on the Allegheny. In 1868 she was owned by Thomas O'Reilly and others.

TRIDENT. A packet built in 1838 at Pittsburgh "expressly for the Allegheny River trade." Capt. Samuel Helvering was her master. Made two trips to Franklin and was sold to the Arkansas River.

TWILIGHT. A towboat built in 1882 at Pittsburgh out of the old *Traveler* by L. Clark. Hull 123 x 13 x 3.9. The history of this boat would fill a book. She had several private owners, then went into the Monongahela River Consolidated Coal & Coke Co., was later the property of the Rodgers Sand Co. and today (1941) is called the *J. H. McCrady*, owned by the McCrady-Rodgers Co., Pittsburgh. She went over Dam 2, Monongahela River about 1913 and sank, was raised. On Oct. 7, 1917, she was running past Braddock, Pa., took a nose dive and sank. Again raised. Nearly burned up on Nov. 15, 1920. Sank near 31st Street, Allegheny River, on Jan. 27, 1921—yet she revived. Although not primarily an Allegheny River towboat, she has seen much service on that stream.

URILDA. A packet new in December, 1863, owned by William S. Evans, D. S. H. Gilmore, and S. S. Coulson. Capt. Thomas W. Laughrey was her master. She ran Ohio River trades in the summer of 1864 and went into the Allegheny River packet trade that fall, Pittsburgh and Oil City. Later she was sold to Capt. Wm. J. Kountz and others and was taken to Missouri River and was commanded by Capt. G. J. Hazlett while there. She was snagged at the foot of Kate Sweeney Bend on April 23, 1869, piloted by Capt. John C. Ball—this on Missouri River.

VENANGO. A packet built in 1857 and came out new in January, 1858, Capt. Thomas H. Reynolds, as part owner and master. Made her trial trip down the Ohio to Sewickley, Pa., and return on January 23rd, then went in the Allegheny River trade, arriving in Franklin on March 23rd on her initial voyage. She has the distinction of bringing out the first shipment of barreled oil from the Oil City regions, consisting of 55 barrels of crude from the William Phillips well and 20 barrels from the Graff well; this was sold to Samuel M. Kier at Pittsburgh for 20 cents a gallon. In the fall of 1861 this boat ran from Kittanning to the oil regions, making connections with trains of the Allegheny Valley Railroad. Capt. Rees Rees became owner of the *Venango* in 1862 and sold her that fall to Cincinnati parties who ran her in low-water trips between that point and Pittsburgh under command of Capt. Carner.

VENTURE. A towboat used on the Allegheny about 1873 owned by J. V. McDonald and others. Capt. A. W. Graham was master.

VIRGINIA. A packet new in May, 1848, owned by George Ledlie of Pittsburgh and commanded by Capt. William T. Dawson. She engaged in low-water trades on the Ohio River and exploded at Rush Run on March 31, 1849, with a loss of ten lives, then in the Steubenville and Wheeling trade. She was repaired and went back to the Allegheny River. In 1851 she was in the Pittsburgh and Catfish trade, Capt. Martin Millinger. He sold her in July that year to Capt. Galloway for the Pittsburgh and Zanesville trade.

W. A. EDDY. This was a side-wheeler, 53 x 10, and built at Cold Spring, N.Y. She came down past Warren, Pa., on April 2, 1870. Had a capacity of 14 tons and carried 50 passengers. Had one boiler and one engine. Her paddles were 2 feet long and 10 inches wide. She went into the Parkers Landing and Foxburg trade, two points great for petroleum production.

WARREN. A packet built at Pittsburgh in 1841 and owned by Morgan M. Hall, Andrew Summerville, William Dale. Capt. Hall was master of her. She was designed for the packet trade between Pittsburgh and Warren, Pa., up the Allegheny. In 1842 her master was Capt. Hugh Harkins and she was owned by Sidney Moreland and Arch Mason. She struck a rock at Nicholsons Falls in May, 1843, and sank, was raised. That fall she ran in the Pittsburgh and Beaver, Pa., trade on the Ohio River, Capt. J. McDonald, along with the *Cleveland* and the *Michigan*. When the Allegheny got back to a navigable stage she returned to her old stand. Backed out of Freeport, Pa., upbound, Dec. 7, 1843, and collapsed a flue, scalding twelve persons badly; some four or five of them died from the effects later. She was repaired and continued in business. Capt. Hugh W. Ward was her master in 1844. In May that year she struck a rock 12 miles below Franklin, downbound, broke in two, sank. Raised and got a new hull and continued in Allegheny River trade until the spring of 1846, when she was caught out on the shore at the Hand Street bridge, Pittsburgh, on a falling river and wrecked. She was replaced by the *Oneota* (which see).

WAVE. A packet built in the spring of 1848 owned by Charles F. Spang and James McAuley. Capt. Ezekiel Gordon was master. She operated between Pittsburgh and Sharpsburg, carrying materials for Spang & Co.'s ironworks. She was sold to Osage River that fall.

WAVE NO. 2. Packet owned by Spang & Co. of Sharpsburg, Pa. Rated at 101 tons and came out new in October, 1848. Capt. William H. Gordon was master. She made many trips as high as Warren, Pa., by reason of her light draft. In the fall of 1850 she was sold to Kanawha

River parties. There is an excellent picture of this boat in the Cincinnati Library at the present time (1941).

WESTERN ENGINEER. A steamboat of 30 tons capacity built at the United States Arsenal, Pittsburgh, on the banks of the Allegheny River and launched on March 28, 1819—the first recorded steamboat built on the Allegheny. She went to the Missouri River under command of Major S. H. Long for the famed Yellowstone Expedition of that time. One unique feature of her construction was a huge serpent head on the stem through which a steampipe was connected from the exhaust of the engine. This could be turned on and it gave the appearance of a dragon breathing fire, much to the astonishment of the Missouri Indians.

WILD BOY. A towboat built in 1865 at Pittsburgh and her first skipper was Capt. A. Inskeep. Rated at 53 tons. Ran on the Allegheny River. She had two boilers and 10's-4 ft. engines. In 1867 her master was Capt. Stephen Rodgers. In 1872 she was still going strong, owned then by A. Culbertson and mastered by Capt. Samuel Culbertson.

WILD DUCK. Towboat built in 1865 and used on the Allegheny during the oil excitement. She had 17's-5½ ft. stroke engines, three boilers. In 1867 she was towing model barges to St. Louis from Pittsburgh, Capt. W. F. Adams, for the Pittsburgh & St. Louis Barge Co. Still in service there in 1869.

WILLIAM BARNHILL. A towboat new in December, 1863, Capt. Richard Mews, and entered Allegheny towing business. In the middle of March, 1864, she struck the old aqueduct bridge pier at Pittsburgh, sank, and lost a barge of empty oil barrels she had in tow; bobbing barrels filled the river. She was raised. She went into the Monongahela River towing trades in the seventies and sank at Lock One, bottom side up, near the Panhandle Bridge at Try Street, then commanded by a Captain Kennedy. She was wrecked, and her engines were used on a new boat.

William D. Duncan. Built at Pittsburgh in the spring of 1828 by A. Mason. Capt. Benjamin Crooks was master. She went up the Allegheny River as far as Franklin, Pa., in 32 hours, arriving there Feb. 24, 1828, being the first steamboat to ascend the Allegheny to that point. She pioneered on up to Oil Creek on the same voyage. Rated at 110 tons. In 1829 she went to the Missouri River.

William Phillips. A packet new in February, 1849, and ran up the Allegheny River commanded by Capt. John McPhail. She ran in the Pittsburgh and Beaver, Pa., trade on the Ohio River that summer and was sold in November to Kanawha River parties and entered the Gallipolis and Kanawha River trade, Capt. Newton, making two round trips a week. Was there in 1850.

W. T. Smoot. Towboat originally built as the *Robert Taylor*. In 1909 she made Allegheny River history by going up to Emlenton, Pa., and operating there some six weeks during the construction of a water-intake pier. She worked for contracting companies until sold to the Water Transport Co. of Pittsburgh in the fall of 1920, and was renamed *Convoy*. Later she was the *A. C. Ingersoll, Jr.* of the Ohio River Co., Huntington; burned Aug. 23, 1940, on the Ohio River below Augusta, Ky.

YANKEE. A packet owned by Capt. William J. Kountz and built in 1847. She was employed on the Allegheny River transferring freight and passengers between Pittsburgh and Freeport when the aqueduct of the Pennsylvania Canal burned on May 13, 1847.

INDEX